Praise for *Letters to a Young*

"Every prospective teacher, education advocate, and education journalist ought to read *Letters to a Young Education Reformer*, the latest wise and evenhanded book by Rick Hess, one of the few true iconoclasts in education reform. I always learn something from his work, and this book—informed by his decades of experience as an educator, policy expert, and also as a parent—is no exception."

—**Dana Goldstein, author,** *The Teacher Wars:*
A History of America's Most Embattled Profession

"Regardless of their political views and commitments, readers will learn much about reform in this important book. It stimulates deep thinking and will surely ignite productive conversations with others who are concerned about a range of school improvement imperatives. Hess offers an impressive array of ideas and policy strategies."

—**Shaun R. Harper, Clifford and Betty Allen Professor,**
University of Southern California Rossier School of Education

"Hess's ability to address complex ideas in simple, conversational language is on full display in this collection of engaging, sometimes poignant personal reflections. Whether his missives usually leave you cheering or fuming, *Letters to a Young Education Reformer* is timely and worth the read, especially his chapter on talking with those who disagree."

—**Stacey Childress, CEO, NewSchools Venture Fund**

"Over the years, there have been many educational issues on which Rick Hess and I have disagreed, but we share a commitment to critically examining issues without being constrained by ideology. In *Letters to a Young Education Reformer*, Hess displays this characteristic openness, offering refreshing insights into controversial policy debates. In this politically polarized climate, his analysis forces readers to consider a range of evidence and opinions as they seek to make a difference in schools today."

—**Pedro A. Noguera, distinguished professor of education,**
Graduate School of Education and Information Sciences,
University of California, Los Angeles

"I can always count on Rick Hess to make me think, and this book is no exception. It will be an important source of insight and motivation for the next generation of scholar-activists in education."

—**Sara Goldrick-Rab, author of *Paying the Price*, and professor of higher education policy, Temple University**

"As both a history lesson and a warning against hubris, *Letters to a Young Education Reformer* reminds the school reform community that the effort is older than the latest group of youthful reformers to join it. Ultimately, it asks reformers of differing motivations and political stripes to come together in the pursuit of great schooling for all of America's children."

—**Derrell Bradford, executive vice president, 50CAN**

"Reading *Letters to a Young Education Reformer* is so many things: encouraging, sobering, affirming, even inspiring. Hess uses what my father calls 'straight talk' to remind educators and those who advocate on their behalf that we must model those basic behaviors that we expect our students to exhibit: respect for the individual, assuming the best, and good listening. His sage and accessible advice is timely as a new generation of leaders moves into position to make a difference in the lives of young Americans and their communities. Practitioners, researchers, policy makers, community leaders, and parents can all benefit from reading this book, discussing it together, and reflecting on what it means for America's children."

—**Irvin Scott, senior lecturer, Harvard Graduate School of Education, and former deputy director, Bill & Melinda Gates Foundation**

"These thought-provoking letters are full of valuable insights for those truly passionate about transforming education. Hess's book is relevant for educators across the political spectrum."

—**Campbell Brown, founder, The 74**

"Current education policy discussions are rarely lacking references to evidence, but they are quite often lacking in wisdom. In *Letters to a Young Education Reformer*, Rick Hess offers readers the wisdom we need to make sense of evidence and use it to improve education. Drawing on his quarter-century of hard experience with education research and practice, the volume offers lessons on a broad range of topics from the Common Core to court-driven reform to the perils of passion. Young and old reformers alike can benefit from his insights."

—Jay P. Greene, distinguished professor of education policy and department head, Department of Education Reform, University of Arkansas, College of Education and Health Professions

"In *Letters to a Young Education Reformer*, Rick Hess reminds us that there is no 'one way' to fix education in America. Rather, by sharing his wisdom, practical perspective, and lessons learned, he challenges each of us to talk less, listen more, and open our minds to the new ideas that could help shape education and learning in our world of tomorrow. I absolutely love this book!"

—Kevin P. Chavous, education reform leader and author of *Building a Learning Culture in America*

"In the decades-long battle of ideas and programs among reformers, this is a refreshing call for greater humility among those trying to improve schools. A former teacher, current policy maven, and parent, Hess offers a personal take on reform and pleads for more collaboration across the political spectrum and a thorough vetting of the 'how' of reform rather than the 'what.' I found *Letters to a Young Education Reformer* to be one of the best reads of the year."

—Larry Cuban, professor emeritus of education, Stanford University

"A must-read for millennials getting ready to make their mark on education. Hess has spent decades working with practitioners, policy makers, and scholars from all sides of the education reform debate. In this book, his personal stories and frank reflections remind us that passion alone will not solve the challenges we face in education. He urges young people to combine their enthusiasm with discipline, thoughtfulness, and humility—a reminder that is relevant to all of us in the education policy world."

—Michelle Reininger, assistant professor and executive director, Center for Education Policy Analysis, Stanford University

Letters to a Young Education Reformer

THE EDUCATIONAL INNOVATIONS SERIES

The Educational Innovations series explores a wide range of current school reform efforts. Individual volumes examine entrepreneurial efforts and unorthodox approaches, highlighting reforms that have met with success and strategies that have attracted widespread attention. The series aims to disrupt the status quo and inject new ideas into contemporary education debates.

Letters to a Young Education Reformer

Frederick M. Hess

HARVARD EDUCATION PRESS
CAMBRIDGE, MASSACHUSETTS

Paperback ISBN 978-1-68253-022-1
Library Edition ISBN 978-1-68253-023-8

Library of Congress Cataloging-in-Publication Data

Names: Hess, Frederick M., author.
Title: Letters to a young education reformer / Frederick M. Hess.
Other titles: Educational innovations.
Description: Cambridge, Massachusetts : Harvard Education Press, [2017] |
  Series: Educational innovations series | Includes bibliographical
  references and index.
Identifiers: LCCN 2016054207| ISBN 9781682530221 (pbk.) | ISBN 9781682530238
  (library edition)
Subjects: LCSH: Educational change—United States. | Educational
  innovations—United States. | Education and state—United States. | School
  management and organization—United States.
Classification: LCC LA217.2 .H484 2017 | DDC 370.973—dc23 LC record available at
  https://lccn.loc.gov/2016054207

Published by Harvard Education Press,
an imprint of the Harvard Education Publishing Group

Harvard Education Press
8 Story Street
Cambridge, MA 02138

Cover Design: Ciano Design
Cover Image: ZOOM(189) Friends-Campus Life/Getty Images

The typeface used in this book is Minion Pro.

For my boys, Guv and Dreamer.
May your schools be palaces
of possibility and learning.

Contents

Preface

IF YOU'VE SPENT MORE THAN five minutes around schools, you've probably got a reflexive reaction to the term *education reformer*. The very phrase tends to spark either cheers or catcalls. You've seen the effusive profiles of heroic charter school leaders who are working wonders. And you've perused the bitter blogs attacking those same leaders as "deformers" bent on destroying public education.

If you're like me, it can all get a little confusing.

In truth, for all the passion, I'm not sure that most of us have all that clear a notion of what it means to be a "reformer." For example, a few years ago, the education advocacy group StudentsFirst leaked a strategy memo. The big takeaway? "Pro-education reform messages resonate strongly with voters and move voter sentiment significantly in favor of pro-reform candidates."[1]

To this day, I don't know what they meant by "pro-education reform" messages or "pro-reform" candidates. I don't think they did, either.

Does a "reformer" have to support charter schools, the Common Core, and the use of test scores to evaluate teachers? Are you a "reformer" if you went through Teach For America or work for a certain kind of advocacy group? Are you "anti-reform" if you have concerns about mayoral control or test-based accountability, or if you fear that some ambitious reforms have done more harm than good?

These questions come up a lot when I'm teaching, talking to educators, or engaging with would-be reformers. For our purposes, I don't care how you answer them. In fact, I don't care about your politics and I'm not interested in telling you *what* to think of this or that reform. This is a book about *how* to think about schooling, policy, and change. It's for anyone who thinks schools can and should do better, in the hope that it will help you work more effectively for the changes that you believe in.

You may champion charter schools or oppose them. You may support test-based accountability or think it's an awful idea. You may want schools to devote far more attention to social and emotional learning or to racial equity, LGBT issues, or children with special needs. Your passion may be teacher empowerment, expanding parental choice, improving gifted education, or overhauling school finance.

Education is brimming with passionate people who see schooling as a way to make a difference. Most of the time, passion is a wonderful thing. It lends us energy and gives our work meaning. In school reform, though, I sometimes think we suffer from a curious malady: too much passion.

The thing about passion is that it tends to make us true believers. It leaves little room for uncertainty. It can make things seem simpler than they are and us more confident in our answers than we should be. It can cause reformers to brush aside second thoughts and to be less than fully honest with ourselves about mistakes and setbacks. Over the years, I've watched impassioned reformers of every stripe stumble in these ways time and again. This is bad for kids, teachers, schools—and frequently, even for reformers' own agendas.

Now, you may be wondering, "Wait a minute! Why should I read on if you're not even going to try to tell me which reforms are the right ones?"

Well, after a quarter-century in education, it seems to me that the notion of the "right" reform is frequently a phantasm. Whether reform is good for kids is often more a matter of what is *actually done* than what policy is officially adopted. Similar-sounding proposals to reform school governance, assessment, discipline, or instruction may turn out to be "right" or "wrong" depending on how they're designed and executed. Reform often disappoints not because the ideas are necessarily "wrong" but because they're pursued in hurried, half-baked ways.

Plus, let's be real. Lots of people are eager to tell you which reforms to support; yet, when I teach, I've found that students have a much harder time finding guidance on how to make sense of reform, why it succeeds or fails, and what lessons reformers might take. Such advice is especially relevant, I think, given that most of us who opine on what needs to be done have unimpressive track records of actually being right.

So my aim is to share some advice on *how* to think about school reform. In the letters that follow, I hope you can benefit from my missteps, frustrations, and realizations. And believe me, I've made my share of mistakes.

In *The Beggar King and the Secret of Happiness*, Joel Ben Izzy tells the tale of Nasrudin's advice to an eager student:

> The student asked, "What is the secret to attaining happiness?"
> Nasrudin thought for a time, then responded. "The secret of happiness is good judgment."
> "Ah," said the student. "But how do we attain good judgment?"
> "From experience," answered Nasrudin.
> "Yes," said the student. "But how do we attain experience?"
> "Bad judgment."[2]

I've always liked that. We're all going to make bad decisions. But we do ourselves a big favor if we draw what wisdom we can from the experiences and bad judgment of others.

And I've got plenty of both to share. During a quarter century in and around school reform, I've spent a lot of time with legislators, philanthropists, federal officials, researchers, and reporters. I've had too many cocktails with two decades' worth of school reform leaders. I've taught at a handful of universities and trained teachers and school and system leaders. I've advised superintendents and start-ups. I've been around for the Annenberg Challenge, the emergence of KIPP and Teach For America, No Child Left Behind, Reading First, the creation of the Institute of Education Sciences, the chancellorships of Joel Klein and Michelle Rhee, *Waiting for Superman*, Race to the Top, the Common Core, the Every Student Succeeds Act, and much else. These letters are my attempt to pass along some of the insights I've gleaned and lessons I've learned.

Before we move on, I want to say a few words about why I wrote this book the way I did.

Why a series of letters? First, many of the topics get personal and pretty subjective. I felt more comfortable sharing my thoughts as a genial correspondent than in a more authoritative voice. Second, in these pages, I'm less interested in making an argument than in exploring the many facets of reform. The casual, open-ended tenor of a correspondence seemed right for the job.

Why are these letters addressed to "young" reformers in particular? Well, most of what follows was inspired by conversations with twenty- and thirty-somethings, in classroom discussions with students at places like Harvard, Rice, and the University of Pennsylvania or in exchanges with educators, philanthropists, advocates, researchers, and reporters.

I've found that young reformers wrestle with certain common dilemmas. They struggle with the political dimension of reform, how to ensure that policies work as intended, and the democratic implications of big philanthropy and school choice. They're interested in figuring out "what works" and can have little patience for opposition or obstacles. The thoughts that follow are intended to help with all of this.

Now, while these letters have been sparked by young reformers, every word applies equally to us not-so-young reformers—as long as we're inclined to confront our biases, blind spots, and bad habits. Over time, we all settle into comfortable assumptions and habits of mind. That can make it tough to dust off our beliefs and revisit our dogmas, but it's extraordinarily healthy to do so.

If you're like the grad students who ask why I'm skeptical of research claiming to prove that merit pay does or doesn't "work," these letters are for you. If you're like the advocates who wonder why their sensible ideas encounter fierce resistance, these letters are for you. If you're like the reporters who wonder why I'm reluctant to name the nation's best school systems, they're for you. If you're like the state and district leaders who wondered why I was lukewarm on *Waiting for Superman*, the *Vergara* lawsuit, or the Common Core, they're for you. If you're like the razor-sharp research assistants I've mentored over the years, these are the riffs you'd hear from me on topics like education history, the importance of listening to those who disagree, and education technology.

Even if you consider yourself a "far-from-young" reformer, I hope you'll find what follows to be well worth your while.

1

Of "Big-*R*" and "Little-*r*" Reform

LET'S START WITH THIS: What do I mean by "reform"?

I'll get there, but I hope you won't mind if I get there in my own time. You see, "school reform" has taken on a very particular meaning in the past decade: reformers are those who support things like charter schooling, accountability, test-based teacher evaluation, and the Common Core.

In earlier eras, other reform orthodoxies have prevailed. A century ago, the list would have included "scientific management," regular testing, sorting students by IQ, and depoliticizing school boards. In the 1980s, it would have included a more demanding high school curriculum, career ladders for teachers, a longer school year, and tougher teacher certification tests.

The problem is that, whatever one thinks of today's reform catalogue, this kind of list *isn't how I define reform*. For me, reform is more a matter of how one thinks about school improvement than a recital of programs and policy proposals.

Given that, I think my take will make more sense if I first say a bit about why I became a "reformer" in the first place.

It's partly because, as a student, a teacher, and a trainer of teachers, I found too many classrooms and schools to be spirit-eroding and mind-numbing. Bells rang, students took their seats, and minutes ticked by. And it's also because I experienced and saw classrooms that were wholly different—places where students felt valued, inspired, and challenged. Most of us picture a particular classroom when we say that. For me, it

1

was sixth grade with Selma Ziff at Pine Ridge Elementary. That year was a whirlwind of math drills, Shakespearean plays, schemes to colonize Mars, and probability learned by gambling with M&Ms. It was a relentless, joyous voyage of discovery and learning. It was what school should be. Hell, it was what *childhood* should be.

For me, reform has never been about anything as high-flown as "social justice" or as prosaic as "workforce readiness." It's been about wanting more classrooms to resemble the ones I loved, and frustration that we weren't making that happen.

It's long seemed clear to me that we can do much better. Better at igniting imagination. At helping students master world languages. At teaching science and history. At instilling a sense of civic responsibility. At ensuring that all students are literate and numerate. At cultivating interest in the arts. At raising kids who are kind and curious. But it's seemed equally clear that doing this will require allowing ourselves to reimagine and rethink schooling.

My own relationship with schools was bittersweet. Ziff's class was the exception, not the rule. I was raised by educated parents, loved reading from an early age, and attended perfectly adequate public schools in New Jersey and terrific ones in Virginia. You'd think that I would've been a safe bet academically. Not so much.

In elementary school, I skipped second grade—a quick fix intended to address my boredom and attendant misbehavior. It didn't take. By high school, I was a consistently lousy student. I was undisciplined, unmotivated, and unconcerned about my prospects. I avoided organized activities, didn't do much homework, studied sporadically, and floundered in any class I didn't like.

Yet I was intrigued by the world around me. I read avidly and broadly. And there were occasions—in a history, government, or English class with the right teacher, or in the three periods of journalism I took in twelfth grade—when flashes of talent or interest would surface. Even at that age, this disconnect struck me as strange.

That sense only deepened when I entered college and found that I had magically morphed into a "good" student. The explanation? I was suddenly free to study only what interested me. Despite some bumps along the way—I missed a couple weeks of class during my sophomore year when I discovered Kurt Vonnegut—it worked out.

That same year, I started substitute teaching for beer money. When I did, I couldn't help noticing how many kids also regarded their school day as time spent in a medium security prison. High schooler Nikhil Goyal captured things pretty pithily in *One Size Does Not Fit All: A Student's Assessment of School*: "I was bored as hell in class and absolutely nothing I was taught was relevant to real life."[1] Given the human mind's innate curiosity and instinct to teach and mentor, I've always found it puzzling that so many of our schools are so at odds with our best nature.

In their avid focus on performance metrics and achievement gaps, contemporary reformers can sometimes seem unbothered that so many students find school so mind-numbing. In my experience, tedium and boredom are rarely front and center except when they're linked to issues of poverty or race. That's nuts. These broad-based frustrations ought to be at the beating heart of reform.

When I entered teaching, I'd catch glimpses of why schools might be so stultifying. I remember applying for my first teaching job in January 1990. I'd graduated summa cum laude from Brandeis University and was earning a teaching credential from Harvard's Graduate School of Education. I felt pretty good about my prospects . . . until I sent letters of inquiry to 130 school districts nationwide and got no responses. I might as well have set the whole sack of letters on fire and tossed them off Boston's Tobin Bridge. I later learned that school districts didn't reply to inquiries until the spring. Why? Because contract provisions and administrative routines dictated that this was how things were done.

I ultimately landed a job in East Baton Rouge Parish, Louisiana, on the basis of a hurried conversation at a cattle call of a recruiting fair. The recruiter had already filled her interview sheet, but she spied my "Harvard" name tag and said, "Sugar, talk to me." Five minutes later, I had my first teaching job. I was hired to teach high school, then assigned to a middle school—and then, days before school started, reassigned to an open position at Scotlandville High School. So much for my careful lesson planning.

I'd been hired, in part, to launch what would have been the third Advanced Placement economics program in the state (*that* would have been a neat trick to pull off in a middle school). It never happened. By the time I was assigned to Scotlandville, it was judged too late to bother. The following year, when I offered to teach AP economics as an extra class during my prep period, I got reprimanded for being a troublemaker. When I offered to pick up a classroom set of introductory economics textbooks for thirty bucks at a Louisiana State University used book sale, I was admonished for asking before I'd submitted the requisite paperwork. I found the school and system to be populated by well-meaning people who spent an extraordinary amount of energy trying not to get in trouble. With time, I learned that my experience was all too typical.

When I left teaching to pursue my doctorate, I returned to Harvard, this time to the political science department. In graduate school, I read and thought deeply about educational politics, policy, and bureaucracy. My dissertation examined when and why districts pursued various reforms. As I studied fifty-seven urban systems, I ran into a serious problem: everyone was doing everything. Over the three years I studied, the average district launched eleven significant reforms—that's one every three months.[2]

Reform was a ceaseless whirlwind that exhausted educators and bred cynicism. Teachers learned to shut their doors while muttering, "This too shall pass." I concluded that reform done poorly is often worse than no reform at all, and that the real challenge is more often one of execution than of action. This was noteworthy in an era when many prominent voices were insisting that what we really needed was to "shake up" urban education.

My thinking proved to be a poor fit for the prevailing orthodoxy in education. When I fretted about things like bureaucracy, perverse incentives, and inept HR systems, I got bemused looks. When I suggested that professional development or differentiated instruction weren't going to make much difference unless we first addressed those organizational problems, I found few who thought similarly.

The search for those who shared my concerns was what led me into the school reform orbit. As I searched, my earlier experiences shaped my views in crucial ways. I was convinced that schools could be soul-deadening for far too many children, and not just for those in poverty. I suspected that what ailed education was as much about bureaucracy as pedagogy, and that many well-intended reforms actually made things worse. I was skeptical that just making education "a priority" would solve any of this, and eager to find people who might see things similarly.

At that time, today's familiar constellation of advocacy groups and charter school operators didn't yet exist. There weren't tens of thousands of Teach For America alumni. There was no NewSchools Venture Fund, Charter School Growth Fund, TNTP, Broad Academy, Education Pioneers, New Leaders, 4.0 Schools, Democrats for Education Reform, 50CAN, Relay Graduate School of Education, Uncommon Schools, Achievement First, Success Academies, High Tech High, Educators4Excellence, Leading Educators, or TeachPlus. There was one nascent KIPP school. Rather than today's organized "reform community," with its big conferences and boldfaced names, there was a loose coalition of educators, state officials, professors, and gadflies.

It was also a very different policy environment. Charter schooling was still new, with advocates scrambling just to convince states to make it legal. Alternative teacher licensure was novel. When it came to K–12 schooling, Washington played a modest role and drew limited attention. And there was less division between reform's "talkers" and "doers," due to a paucity of full-time advocates and the fact that many reformers had day jobs.

As I write this, I realize that it sounds like I'm saying school reform began when I arrived. Let me correct myself: generation upon generation of reform predated me. Each wave peaked, crashed, tossed up detritus, and then gave way to the next. Schooling was not bereft of "reformers" when I showed up, though they had different names and goals than today's marquee players.

But because we're each the hero of our own story, it's easy to forget all that happened before we arrived. So, while I knew the 1980s and early 1990s were marked by ambitious fights to change policy and practice, I reflexively discounted them as ancient history. I thought of those fights as a closed book rather than as an earlier chapter in the current one. That was a mistake. It made me think some ideas were novel no-brainers, when more backstory might have given me pause. It meant I missed lessons that I should have learned, misunderstood motives, and dismissed as opponents people who could have been allies.

But I digress; let's get on with the story. When I arrived on the scene, school reform felt different than it does today, and not just because the key players were different. Social media didn't exist. People went to libraries to get the facts on school spending or student achievement. Rather than e-mailing popular news articles, advocates photocopied and sent them via snail mail. There were fewer studies and opinion pieces flying around. This all made for a slower pace, with less noise and a less combative environment.

I tell you this not to bore you with recollections of yesteryear but to give some context for how the world of reform has evolved. In the past two decades, reformers have enjoyed some remarkable success. Along the way, they have acquired some new habits, good and bad.

For me, an early lesson about those bad habits came in late 2002. I had just given up my professorship at the University of Virginia to move to Washington and launch the education policy studies program at the American Enterprise Institute (AEI). At the time, in the aftermath of 9/11, the United States was in a standoff with Saddam Hussein. We had already invaded Afghanistan, and there was a growing sense that Iraq might be next. I got a phone call from the Department of Defense. They were quietly assembling three-person teams to oversee the various components of the Iraqi government after an invasion, and they were hoping I'd be willing to help with the Ministry of Education.

I was intrigued. I agreed to attend a private briefing at the Pentagon. There were about eight or ten of us in the room—the handful who would oversee the Ministry and a few staff from the armed forces and the administration. As the briefing unfolded, it was clear how little anyone knew. The military team had no clue how many schools would still be standing after an invasion or how many teachers would be willing to go back to work. And none of the projected advisers (including me) spoke the relevant tongues or had any expertise in Iraq or the Middle East.

I gently asked, "You all know I'm Jewish, right? Does that pose any concern?"

A couple of the briefers exchanged glances. One made a hurried note on his pad. Another cleared her throat. It was apparent that they hadn't known and weren't sure. One of them said, "That's good to know. We'll take it under advisement."

I had no idea what that meant.

Meanwhile, one issue dominated that planning session and the next: the notion that the educational priority for post-invasion Iraq would be implementing Iraq's own version of No Child Left Behind (NCLB). Not that we had any clue what kinds of tests Iraq used or much understanding of the Iraqi educational system—or even what percentage of children regularly attended school. But NCLB was the pride and joy of the Bush administration and, boy, was there a desire to use it.

I recall the glower I got from an administration staffer when I asked, "Are we sure that this is something we should be talking about at this stage?" If I could have read her mind, I'm pretty sure she was thinking "Troublemaker." And not in a good way.

I wound up passing on the invitation, but noted how easy it is to fall in love with our enthusiasms, even when they are an awkward fit for the problem at hand. In recent years, I've occasionally flashed back to that experience as I've watched this or that group of reformers settle on an agenda and then dismiss doubters as troublemakers.

This mindset is a problem. It encourages groupthink. It dictates that everyone should seek to "blow up" schools of education or embrace the firm discipline of "no excuses" charter schools—until the reform zeitgeist shifts. Then everyone is supposed to pivot and cheer "reform-minded" education schools or denounce unduly rigid disciplinary policies. The swiftness of these swings can be Orwellian.

Speaking of NCLB reminds me of another formative experience, courtesy of a conference that my friend Checker Finn and I hosted in 2006. The day was devoted to new research examining NCLB's required remedies for schools "in need of improvement." Two moments stood out.

One was a brief exchange regarding schools in need of "corrective action." Researchers had presented glum accounts of how school restructuring was faring. Then two respected officials—California's secretary of education and Florida's commissioner of education—discussed their experiences. California's secretary had been a hard-charging, nontraditional superintendent in San Diego before agreeing to serve under Governor Arnold Schwarzenegger. Nobody ever accused this guy of being soft. Yet he noted resignedly that, for all the law's assurances, all his state's resources, and all the experts he'd consulted, he wasn't sure we actually knew how to turn around troubled schools.

His counterpart was asked, "How many turnarounds can you handle in Florida?" Florida's chief was the no-nonsense, veteran leader of a state then widely regarded as a national school reform exemplar. He said, "Keep in mind that we've got several thousand schools." He paused. "You're just talking about the state department? I'd say we can manage about seven schools." The room's audible shock and disappointment would've been funny in other circumstances.

The second moment involved the day's final panel. The session featured a few prominent thinkers on federal policy, including historian Diane Ravitch. After decades championing test-based accountability and school choice, Ravitch was starting to reverse her views. That day, responding to the bleak portrayal of NCLB's school improvement efforts, Ravitch aptly captured the crowd's disquiet, saying it was clear that the law had big problems. She would later point to that conference as one experience that helped convince her that accountability and choice don't work.

Ravitch got some important things right, but I fear she learned the wrong lessons. She was right that the federally mandated remedies were generally ineffectual, that reformers had oversold the wonders of accountability, and that strategies like charter schooling aren't a "fix" for struggling schools. Her mistake, though, was to conclude that accountability and choice "don't work." Indeed, she was making a version of the mistake she had made in the 1990s (and that many reformers continue to make), when she had insisted that choice and accountability do indeed "work."

Policies like choice and accountability can help, but they can also hurt. They're not elixirs. They can help to empower parents and educators and to foster coherent school communities, but they can also have much less salutary effects. In any event, they *don't make kids learn*. They are not instructional interventions, like reading programs or pedagogical techniques. What they can do is help *create the conditions* for improvement. Unfortunately, reformers have long treated the complexities of change as less interesting or important than the battles to win that change. The backlash Ravitch helped spark has been one understandable, if unfortunate, consequence.

All of this is to say that reform isn't just about having good ideas. It's about figuring out how to make those ideas actually work. This can be a hard lesson to learn. It means reformers need to sweat things like perverse incentives and whether a policy is likely to actually, you know, work as intended, even when they'd rather focus on moral exhortation or larger causes. It means thinking about how reforms will affect the day-to-day lives of students, families, and educators. It means grasping why teacher recruitment strategies that work great in highly educated coastal cities may not work as well in struggling Midwestern towns. It can seem like good ideas and good intentions should count for more. But they don't. Sorry.

With all that by way of prelude, let's return to my opening question: What do I mean by "reform"?

First, reform is about system change. It's about changing state or federal policy, school district behaviors, or routines and practices on a sweeping scale. It's not a teacher launching a program or a school extending its day. Those things are isolated changes to practice. Now, in no way am I saying that "reform" is more important than these changes to practice. I am saying that it's *different*, and that the difference is important.

To me, reform is mostly a matter of opening up outdated systems so that educators, entrepreneurs, parents, and communities can reinvent schooling to better educate every child. I'm more interested in stripping away anachronistic policies and empowering educators than in imposing my preferred practices and programs. That's because I think the best-designed and most promising solutions will come from educators and entrepreneurs on the ground, not from reformers ensconced in office buildings in state capitals or Washington, DC. I see reform less as a roster of fixes and more as a dynamic process of reinvention, evolution, and support for those doing the work.

When making sense of the reform landscape, I find it convenient to distinguish between what I think of as "big-*R*" Reform and "little-*r*" reform. Over time, we've adopted the habit of branding a very specific bundle of policies as "Reform" (with a capital *R*). In the past decade or so, big-*R* Reform has generally referred to test-based accountability, charter schooling, the Common Core, new teacher evaluation systems, mandatory school turnaround strategies, and support for a sizable federal role in schooling.

Little-*r* reform, on the other hand, is more a set of precepts than policy prescriptions. Little-*r* reformers agree that schools can do a far better job of imparting knowledge, forming citizens, stimulating minds, and cultivating great teaching. They believe that schooling needs to be reimagined and that this requires remaking or removing many old systems and policies. They believe that educators should be accountable and that excellence should be rewarded, but that there are many ways to do these things. Little-*r* reformers are far less confident than big-*R* Reformers that they know the right solutions or understand the full impact of policy changes.

What's the relationship between big-*R* and little-*r* reform? They can sound like opposites, but it's fairer to say that big-*R* Reform is an *offshoot* of little-*r* reform. Little-*r* reform presumes that we need to rethink schools and schooling, while big-*R* Reform offers a particular agenda for doing so. Over time, as big-*R* Reform has congealed into a set of prescriptions, it has grown more bureaucratic, more self-assured, and further and further removed from the intuitions of little-*r* reform. This has been unfortunate, but hardly unprecedented.

I'll tell you flat-out that I'm a little-*r* reformer.

My kind of reform embraces a set of broad principles: Those making decisions should be responsible for making them work and also for the consequences. This means that more authority should rest with accountable educators and less with state and federal officials. Bureaucratic routine is a lousy way to cultivate great schools. Policy can make people do things, but it can't make them do them well—and when it comes to schooling, what usually matters is *how* things are done rather than *whether* they're done.

And, perhaps most crucially, *each of these principles can be brought to life in a lot of different ways.* These principles don't amount to a specific agenda; to my mind, that's a feature, not a flaw. It invites lots of possible solutions and healthy discussion. Washington-centric, dogmatic big-*R* Reform has too often neglected this reality, with reformers exhausting themselves to win policy fights and then winding up too bloodied and battered to make those wins matter. It's left me to wonder whether all the fuss and furor of recent years has done more harm than good.

My brand of little-*r* reform is a big-tent and small-*d* democratic vision of reform. I choose to regard those who share my frustrations, aspirations, and beliefs as fellow reformers, whether or not they agree with me on charter schooling, teacher licensure, school discipline, or accountability. This has allowed me to connect with and learn from those who might agree in spirit but disagree on important particulars. I think that's healthy.

I hope the letters ahead just might help inform your aims and assumptions as you and your colleagues set out to write the next chapter of education reform.

2

Talkers and Doers

IN 2015, I PENNED *The Cage-Busting Teacher*. Over the years, even terrific teachers had routinely told me how stifled they felt by school systems that ignored their input, subjected them to mindless professional development, and bombarded them with new directives. They told me of shutting their doors, keeping their heads down, and doing their best to tune out distractions. In writing that book, I hoped to help those teachers understand how they could make school systems and policy work for them rather than against them.

One big step, I noted then, was playing nicer with administrators, policymakers, and advocates. I'd heard too many teachers grumble about central office knuckleheads and read too many teachers' blogs about the "war" on public education. I told teachers, "You're not going to get much of a hearing from leaders and reformers if you keep ripping into them. If you want them to work with you, you need to listen to them and try to work with them."

A lot of teachers replied, "Okay, but how come this is all on us? Don't they have an obligation to listen to us and work with us?"

Damn right they do. And the truth is that reformers have generally done pretty miserably on this count. That helps explain why school reform sometimes resembles a World War I battlefield. Reformers blast teachers as incompetent and schools as failing. Teachers react angrily, dismissing reform as an attack on their schools and their profession. Then everyone settles back into their trenches and prepares for the next clash.

As one educator put it, "I'm sick to death of being told my business by some twenty-six-year-old who taught for one year and runs around saying our schools are failing. If he knows so damn much, why doesn't he come and teach me his secrets? Because it looks to me like those reformers are out there giving talks while I'm in here doing the work."

I've got a lot of sympathy for that complaint. Educators who rail against reform *do* need to spend less time griping and more time offering practical suggestions. But reformers need to stop giving the impression that they think school improvement is mostly a matter of big plans and policies— and that educators ought to just hush.

Both sides have a point. It's just that they're viewing things through different lenses. Today's big-*R* Reformers, for instance, mostly view schools as a way to promote sweeping social ambitions: reducing poverty, increasing employment, ending injustice. They're less concerned with the culture of a given school or what educators think is reasonable than with measurable results. If they have to break a few eggs, so be it.

Educators, on the other hand, spend every day in schools. They think granularly—in terms of individual students, curricular units, and instructional strategies. Most think that they're doing the best they can, and that their best is pretty good. Educators are deeply versed in the fabric of schooling, worry about the unintended consequences of reforms, and feel like reformers are scapegoating them for society's ills.

It's okay, even healthy, that reformers and practitioners see things differently. Educators are looking from the inside out, and reformers from the outside in.

In all walks of life, there are doers and there are talkers. Their different perspectives and priorities can work in concert. Doers are the people who teach students, arrest murderers, fix plumbing, and make balloon animals. Talkers are the people who survey the sweep of what's being done and talk about ways to do it better.

If someone is a big-*R* Reformer, there's a good chance he or she's a talker. If someone works for an advocacy group, website, activist organization, consulting firm, university, research shop, think tank, foundation, or government agency, it's a safe bet that person's a talker.

It's fine to be a talker. I'm one, too. Talkers have an important role to play, as long as they keep in mind it's the doers who are actually, you know, doing things.

In education, plenty of talkers used to be doers. But that doesn't change the logic of the situation. It's great if an NFL commentator used to play pro football. But it doesn't change the fact that he's opining from an air-conditioned booth while the players are out there sweating and tackling. As President Theodore Roosevelt eloquently put it more than a century ago, "It is not the critic who counts; not the man who points out how the strong man stumbles, or where the doer of deeds could have done them better. The credit belongs to the man who is actually in the arena, whose face is marred by dust and sweat and blood."[1]

The symbiosis between doers and talkers has gotten lost. The fault for this lies with both sides. Yet some big-R Reformers seem bent on making things worse by regarding tough talk as a badge of honor and reflexively dismissing teacher complaints. When I've written about why some goofy accountability or teacher evaluation policies infuriate good teachers, more than a few big-R Reformers have shaken their heads and told me that I've "gone soft."

When *The Cage-Busting Teacher* was published, a number of reformers were curious about what the teachers I'd interviewed had to say. When we'd talk, though, they tended to hear only the bits that they found congenial. I remember one senior foundation official who said, "You're so right about needing to respect the doers" and agreed that reformers needed to focus more intently on how their proposals affect educators. Then he added, "But I worry that this can all distract from getting the policies right." I did a face-palm. The whole point is that policies are only "right" if they enable doers to do the work better.

There are times when talkers' self-regard can get truly farcical. One of my all-time favorite examples was when the Oregon School Boards Association detailed the myriad ways educators and students could celebrate "School Board Recognition Month." Given that a quarter of the state's students were chronically absent at the time, you'd be forgiven for thinking that board members should have had more important things on their minds. But the Oregon School Boards Association wanted students and teachers to put a *lot* of energy into honoring those board members. Their lengthy list of suggestions included having students "laminate place mats autographed by the class for each board member," "make cookies or goodies and deliver them to board members at their place of employment," and "create gifts of potted plants or floral arrangements" in horticulture class.[2] This is what happens when talkers forget their role.

To avoid that, there are a few things that talkers need to keep in mind.

First, talkers don't educate kids and aren't held accountable for whether students are learning. So it's no real surprise that educators see talkers as backseat drivers. Now, passengers can see things the driver can't, studying alternate routes on the GPS or spotting a road closure sign that the driver missed. But passengers also need to recognize all the stuff they're not dealing with because *they're not driving.* There's a reason that nobody likes backseat drivers, even when the advice is sound.

Second, talkers need to become better listeners. I have no patience for educators who want policy makers to "get out of schooling." Public schools are funded with public taxes to serve the public's kids. That means that public officials will—and should—have plenty to say. But public officials and other talkers have a reciprocal obligation to listen to educators and to learn from them. Educators are the ones who see how new evaluation systems, state tests, or interventions really play out. Listening to them requires more than talking to union officials or the leaders of teacher advocacy groups who show up at conferences; it means seeking perspectives from a cross-section of practitioners.

Third, listening to educators *does not* mean pandering to them. There's an unfortunate tendency to talk to educators like they're Girl Scouts: They're awesome! They're wonderful! We're so proud of them—now won't they please go play quietly while the adults deal with the serious stuff? Both parts of that formulation are wrong. Reformers can and should say that some teachers are terrific . . . and that some aren't. They should engage doers as adults able to hear both the good and the bad, and expect the same in return. If some doers don't respond in kind, then work with those who will.

There's a moment from my doctoral studies that's long colored how I think about the reformer-teacher relationship. It was a sunny summer day after my first year at Harvard and I was walking to Widener Library. A senior professor fell into step alongside me. At one point, he looked around and sighed. "Rick," he confided, "this place is wonderful when the students aren't here."

I've found that to be a window into how a lot of faculty think about universities. I've also found it a pretty decent metaphor for how some big-R Reformers think about schools: they'd be wonderful places if not for all those inept educators who keep mucking things up. Big-R Reformers have drifted into the unfortunate habit of talking a lot more about getting rid of lousy teachers than giving excellence its due.

There's a larger point here. Ultimately, reform should be profoundly pro-teacher. When reformers wax eloquent about students trapped in dysfunctional schools and systems, they sometimes forget that many teachers feel equally trapped. The same bureaucracy and ineptitude that frustrate reformers infuriate and demoralize the teachers who live with them every day. When reformers ask how their efforts will empower responsible doers, they invite a partnership that's good for talkers, doers, and, most of all, students.

Talkers and doers need each other. Educators see when policies misfire, how funding mandates cause headaches, and where support services come up short. Talkers have the time to study policy proposals, build relationships with policy makers, and master the big picture. They have the distance to raise hard truths that can be uncomfortable for educators to address because they strike so close to home. Together, talkers and doers can accomplish great things. The question is whether they're up for the challenge.

3

The Value in Talking with Those Who Disagree

A FEW YEARS AGO, I was teaching a graduate seminar in education policy at the University of Pennsylvania. The topic was charter schooling. The students, mostly veteran school and system leaders, got into a heated discussion. About half the class regarded charters as a no-brainer, as something that any reasonable person should support. They couldn't figure out why their classmates didn't get it.

Meanwhile, the other half of the class couldn't figure out what *their* classmates were thinking. One charter critic declared, "You're ignoring the research. Charter schools get worse results and are more segregated than public schools, even though they get to choose their students. What about this sounds like a good idea to you?"

The classmate she was addressing looked dumbfounded. He spluttered, "That's totally wrong. How can you say that? The research shows that charters do better than district schools. Charters don't skim the easy-to-educate kids. If anything, they're serving low-income families. And they're doing it with less money."

The conversation ground to an exasperated standstill. In frustration, someone finally asked me, "Why do we keep disagreeing on the facts here? Seems like there should be studies that settle this."

I put the question to them: *How can smart, informed people look at the same facts and see them so differently?*

The answer is pretty simple. People are different. We value different things. We fear different things. We interpret the same bits of evidence differently. When we peer into the same basket of facts, we pull out different ones and understand them in different ways.

Two people may read about a college graduate struggling with loans. One sees an overburdened victim of a broken system. The other sees an irresponsible slacker with extravagant habits. Who's right? It could well be that they both are. How one answers that question depends on which facts one finds salient and how one interprets them.

A pair of scholars can examine data on racial disparities in AP enrollment rates and come to different conclusions. One sees clear evidence of bias. The other sees an unremarkable reflection of differences in student preparation. The two can look at the exact same data and *still disagree on what they mean.*

In practice, though, we're frequently not looking at the same data. When we read magazines, websites, blogs, and social media, we tend to choose those that reflect and reinforce our biases. About 50 to 60 percent of those who identify as consistently conservative or liberal agree that "most of my close friends share my political views."[1]

We can wind up with limited, truncated views of the world—and not even realize it.

That's a problem. It's especially so when it means that two thoughtful people can read the same things and then talk past one another. That's what happened in my UPenn class that day. What I told the students was that their frustration was the strongest argument I know for valuing diversity. I don't mean "diversity" the way we usually talk about it, which is mostly in terms of skin color and ethnicity. I mean diversity of views, values, attitudes, perspectives, and mind-sets. Race is an important part of this, but so are things like life experience, profession, knowledge, religion, upbringing, and temperament.

Diversity can be as simple as geography. People who've grown up in Berkeley, California, or Birmingham, Alabama, have had different experiences and been exposed to different rhythms and views. That's important because it's only human to imagine that our own biases are normal and that others' are goofy or parochial. That's especially true when we're surrounded by like-minded people. As sportscaster John Buccigross put it, "The closer you physically are to something, the more important it seems . . . You can't work and live in New England and be immune to the fervor of the Boston Red Sox."[2]

There's one anecdote I've always liked because it shows how geography can shape our thinking in all kinds of ways. In college, I spent a summer hitchhiking across the United States. In Birmingham, I spent the night at the Salvation Army alongside fifty homeless men. I passed the better part of the evening chatting with the shift supervisor, a guy who'd just spent several years on a mission abroad. He was curious about my travels, and he and the regulars seemed to find a college student out of Boston interesting and unusual. A month later, I was in a similar venue in Berkeley, where a hitchhiking collegian turned out to be trite and sigh-inducing. When I asked the aging hipster in charge how to get to a couple of landmarks, he looked up wearily and said, "I'll tell you on one condition. Please, please promise not to tell me about your journey or how you're here to find yourself." Our communities, geographic and otherwise, play a powerful role in shaping how we see the world.

Scott Page is a University of Michigan professor who has made a career of studying diversity. In his book *The Difference: How the Power of Diversity Creates Better Groups, Firms, Schools, and Societies*, he explains, "The best problem solvers tend to be similar; therefore, a collection of the best problem solvers performs little better than any one of them individually. A collection of random, but intelligent, problem solvers tends to be diverse. This diversity allows them to be collectively better. Or to put it more provocatively: *diversity trumps ability*."[3] A group of like-minded "smart" people can be undone by their difficulty accounting for—or even acknowledging—facts that don't conform to their worldview.

If you're not inclined to parse Page's mathematical proofs, consider his tale of the famous 1999 chess match involving world champion Garry Kasparov. Event sponsor MSN.com introduced a wrinkle: Kasparov's opponent was actually fifty thousand other players who collectively voted on moves suggested by a small collection of young chess masters. It took the world champ sixty-two exhausting moves to beat the combined wisdom of this non-expert crowd. Page notes, "The collection of people performed far better than would be expected of any of its members individually."[4]

I said above that racial diversity is only a part of what diversity entails, but it's an important part. Members of racially diverse mock juries, for instance, deliberate longer and consider more information than do more homogenous ones. They raise more facts, make about half as many factual errors, and are more open to discussing matters related to race.[5] Engaging those who see things differently can help spare us from critical mistakes.

A half-century ago, in the study that birthed the term *groupthink*, Yale University psychologist Irving Janis observed that the military and civilian leaders blindsided by Pearl Harbor, the Bay of Pigs invasion, the Vietnam War escalation, and the Korean War stalemate had allowed crucial concerns and warning signs to be drowned out by consensus. He observed, "The more amiability and esprit de corps there is," the more likely it is that "independent critical thinking will be replaced by groupthink."[6]

This is all more than a little relevant for school reformers, who tend to work with and listen to people they know, like, and trust. And the costs of groupthink are especially high for them, given the practical complexities and political dimensions of their work. Talking to those who will illuminate blind spots and offer new perspectives isn't a luxury; it's part of the job description.

Yet school reformers have generally done a poor job on this count. Even in organizations that tout their commitment to racial or gender diversity, I frequently encounter astonishing homogeneity in terms of thought and experience. Almost everyone is young. Almost everyone went to a selective college—and a surprising number to the *same* small set of colleges. Almost everyone is focused on closing achievement gaps, wants the federal government to spend more on social programs, and thinks that "the rich" should pay higher taxes. Many entered education through Teach For America and share common formative experiences. The result is an extraordinary amount of like-mindedness regarding what needs to be done and how to do it.

If you mostly talk to people who agree with you, it can be hard to understand why anyone would disagree. You can fall into assuming that dissenters are misguided, ignorant, or malicious. That makes it hard to connect with them, find common ground, or sway their views. And it means you're really, really unlikely to have second thoughts or revisit your assumptions.

I'm not suggesting anything radical. There are obviously people with whom we are never going to agree. There are truly evil people in the world. In education, though, the happy fact is that most of those with whom we disagree are people we'd regard as decent and reasonable if we met them at a Little League game or a coffee shop—we just disagree about pedagogy, school choice, testing, or other fairly refined questions. This means it's worth exploring why we see things differently and what we might learn from one another.

In recent years, though, many on both sides of the reform debates have treated one another as malicious evildoers. They have adopted former President George W. Bush's post-9/11 refrain: "You're either with us, or you're against us." If you're on the team, you pipe down, express any doubts quietly and privately, and sing from the group hymnal.

A 2008 *Yale Alumni Magazine* article quotes Colonel Stephen Gerras, a professor at the US Army War College, explaining the problem of groupthink. Gerras observed that army culture is so "susceptible to groupthink" that there's even an analogy for it—"the bus to Abilene":

> Any army officer can tell you what that means. It came originally from an article by a civilian management researcher. It's now a management training video, and every officer has watched it at least three times by the time they get to the War College. It's about a family sitting on a porch in Texas on a hot summer day, and somebody says, "I'm bored. Why don't we go to Abilene?" When they get to Abilene, somebody says, "You know, I didn't really want to go." And the next person says, "I didn't want to go—I thought you wanted to go."[7]

That story will have an uncomfortable resonance for anyone who's spent enough time around education reform. Look, we may be destined to wind up on that bus to Abilene every once in a while. But we can ensure that the ride is a funny anecdote, and not a regular habit, if we talk and listen to one another before clambering aboard and taking our seats.

4

The Limits of Policy

I'VE SPENT MOST OF MY CAREER thinking about education politics and policy. This means I've spent a lot of time studying once-promising reforms that fell flat. Talk about a crash course in humility.

Don't get me wrong. I'm a big fan of policy. Our schools and systems aren't built for what we're asking them to do today. Doing something about that requires big changes to policies governing staffing, spending, and much else. That's why I'm a school reformer. But policy is better at facilitating that kind of rethinking than at forcing it.

A case in point: In recent years, big-*R* Reformers have pushed states to adopt more rigorous teacher evaluation systems. Their go-to talking point emerged from The New Teacher Project's 2009 study *The Widget Effect*, which reported that more than 99 percent of teachers across the nation were routinely rated "satisfactory."[1] That was true even in school districts with abysmal student performance, and even though teachers themselves report that 5 percent of their colleagues deserve an "F" for their performance.[2]

In Florida, when the governor signed into law landmark reforms to teacher evaluation and pay in 2011, one prominent observer enthused, "Exceptional teachers will now be distinguished, celebrated and rewarded for their dedication and skill."[3]

The Florida reforms mandated that all teachers be evaluated on a set of formal classroom observations and student test gains (in every subject and grade). After a fierce fight for the new law, tens of thousands of hours spent observing and documenting teacher performance, and tens of millions of dollars spent on developing tests, the first year results were issued—and 97 percent of Florida teachers were rated effective.

That wasn't unique to Florida, nor was it a one-time thing. In 2016, researchers Matt Kraft and Allison Gilmour examined teacher evaluation results in nineteen states that adopted new evaluation systems after 2009 and found that, on average, 97 percent of teachers were rated effective. An enormous investment of time, energy, and money had yielded remarkably little change.[4]

It turns out that legislators can change evaluation policies but can't force schools or systems to apply them rigorously or meaningfully. Even several years after policies were changed, Kraft and Gilmour reported that principals remained unsure of what poor teaching looked like, didn't want to upset their staffs, and didn't think giving a negative evaluation was worth the hassle. The result: they didn't bother to give negative evaluations.

A reasonable observer could conclude that the idea "doesn't work" and that the costs of teacher evaluation outweigh any benefits. While I think that's the wrong lesson to draw, it's an understandable reaction. And this is how policy lapses undermine reform. Grand disappointments poison the well for more measured attempts.

And those more measured attempts can yield promising results. In Washington, DC, for instance, an aggressive, carefully crafted teacher evaluation system has worked remarkably well. It's earned the support of educators and benefited from frequent adjustments based on careful analysis and teacher feedback. This is possible when the superintendent is responsible for how the system works, is free to modify it, and can adjust timelines to reflect local realities. That's all far more difficult when dealing with policy directives issued from a state capital, much less from Washington.

The lesson: Policy can make people do things, but it can't make them do them well. Policy is a blunt tool that works best when making people do things is enough. That's why it works reasonably well if the task is issuing Social Security checks, setting noise ordinances, or requiring drivers to have licenses.

In education, policy is mostly likely to work as intended when dealing with "musts" and "must nots," as with things like compulsory attendance, class-size limits, and graduation requirements. Policy is far less effective when it comes to complex endeavors where *how* things are done matters more than *whether* they're done. This is because policy can't make schools or systems adopt reforms wisely or well.

Equipped with only this blunt instrument, though, public officials face enormous pressure to make the world a better place.

Imagine that a state legislator recently visited a school with a terrific new teacher induction program and now wants to ensure that other schools offer something similar. What can she do? Well, she can require that all schools adopt a new teacher induction program. Of course, while some schools may do it enthusiastically and well, the schools she's most concerned about may not take it seriously. So she includes a provision that requires that all schools hold a new teacher orientation session and assign a mentor to each new teacher.

But our legislator fears that the recalcitrant schools will treat the meeting as a joke and the mentoring as busywork. So she includes a provision that requires the orientation to cover eleven specified topics and another requiring mentors to meet weekly with their charges and to fill out a two-page report on each session. By this point, even though the requirements may start to strike some early supporters as excessive and too rigid, they're still not enough to ensure that the orientations will be meaningful or that mentors will treat their weekly meetings and reports as more than box-checking. So she includes a provision . . .

You see the problem.

This is why public education can seem like it's swimming in rules. Every time I speak to teacher leaders, someone invariably asks, "Why does [person X or group Y] think it's a good idea to make so many stupid rules?" Rebecca Mieliwocki, the 2012 national teacher of the year, put it well: "All of this ridiculous administrivia just shows a lack of faith. I tell my administration it's ridiculous to have a check point for every [professional development] session. They tell me, 'You don't understand. Not every teacher is as committed as you are. . .' I told them it sounds like a personnel issue they should handle one-on-one. They said to me, 'Oh, Rebecca. If only you knew.'"[5]

Here's the thing: rules are purposefully written to stop stupidity and malfeasance. As they say in Silicon Valley, "That's not a bug; it's a feature." Policymakers can't make rules that apply only to bad actors, but they can write rules to keep those bad actors in line. And then those rules necessarily apply to everyone, good and bad alike.

Policy often seems dumb to those who are competent and responsible precisely because policies *aren't written for them*. The reason that policy often seems like a series of intrusive mandates and prohibitions is because that's precisely what it is. If teachers get leeway over how to spend professional development funds and a single teacher spends them on a dubious seminar in Cabo, lawmakers are expected to "do something." They do that by adding new restrictions, prohibitions, and directives.

A veteran US Senate staffer once sighed to me, "I see educators who are doing great things in schools and systems. I want to write the rules for them. But I have to write the rules for the lowest common denominator." Why is that?

Well, during the Enlightenment, democratic reformers fought to ensure that laws applied universally and uniformly. Previously, kings had shown an unpleasant inclination to rewrite laws so that they, their families, and their friends could do as they liked. In 1527, England's King Henry VIII wanted to divorce his first wife and marry his lover, Anne Boleyn. When the pope refused to grant the divorce, the king ordered the Archbishop of Canterbury to do it (founding the Church of England in the process). At a time when kings could start religions for their personal convenience, it's no surprise that they altered or ignored laws to punish enemies or reward supporters. The uniform application of law is a blessing in countless ways, but it does have a price.

Even when federal or state officials adopt reasoned policies and local educators want to cooperate, things can go wrong. In *The Cage-Busting Teacher*, I quote former US teaching ambassador fellow Tammie Schrader, who observed,

> I've had the opportunity to sit in the US Department of Education. I see them listening, being thoughtful, and really trying to make good decisions . . . But they don't know what they don't know. And what they just can't know is how that policy will play out in a classroom. The feds might craft a smart, sensible policy. But then the state gets that policy, and they have a whole team of people that tries to decipher and apply it. Then that information goes down to districts, where folks try to decipher and apply it. Then it goes to principals. By the time it hits my classroom, it looks like something that makes no sense at all for kids.[6]

Far too often, in fact, policy unfolds like a children's game of telephone. In Washington, federal officials have a clear vision of what they think a change in guidance on Title I spending should mean. But when officials in fifty states read that new guidance, they don't all understand it the same way. Those officials have to explain it to thousands of district Title I directors, who then translate it for school leaders and teachers. By that point, there's a lot of confusion, fear of getting crosswise with federal law, and half-hearted compliance. Now multiply that a hundredfold for the deluge of state and federal laws and regulations that rain down. This isn't anyone's recipe for dynamic, coherent schools.

And that's all assuming that policy turns out as hoped. That's not always a safe bet. Heck, my very first experience with federal policy was a cautionary one. Back in 2001, I penned a paper titled "Tear Down This Wall" for the Progressive Policy Institute. I argued that we ought to require fewer paper credentials before prospective teachers could apply for a job.[7] The paper received a lot of attention. I was invited to talk about it at the White House, and the US Secretary of Education touted it while Congress was negotiating No Child Left Behind. All good, right? Well, by the time the legislative dust had settled, my suggestion had gotten subsumed in the decision to add a new "highly qualified teacher" provision to the law. So, if anything, I contributed just a bit to Washington making paper credentials even *more* of a requirement. Whoops.

You're probably thinking, "But what about the ways in which policy can catalyze reform—especially the way Washington can give political cover to state and district leaders?" That's a fair point. In the short term, Washington can prod states and districts to adopt certain policies. It can provide "cover" that permits superintendents or state leaders to justify unpopular moves by saying, "I hate to do this, but my hands are tied." And it's always possible that this kind of federal cajoling can deliver lasting change in schooling, as it has with the drinking age or Medicaid expansion. Notice, though, that raising the drinking age and expanding Medicaid eligibility are cases where simply *adopting* the policy is pretty much the whole ballgame. School reform presents profoundly different challenges.

That's why, unfortunately, "cover" has proven a dubious formula for school reformers. It makes for hasty moves on political timelines, a recipe that's better for producing excited headlines than sustained change. It fuels missteps, as reform-minded officials overestimate what their state is willing or prepared to do well. It can cause reformers to skimp on cultivating local support, eroding the backing needed to execute or sustain reform. With the 2009 federal Race to the Top program, for instance, Uncle Sam encouraged well-meaning state officials to move so hurriedly and aggressively that some drove the school reform bus off a cliff. "Cover" is one of those notions that sounds good but frequently hurts reform more than it helps.

When policies don't quite work as hoped, reformers have an unlovely habit of acting as if no one could have anticipated the challenges that bedevil them. Sounding a lot like a kid who leaves his new bike outside and unlocked, and then gets furious when it's stolen, they blame their frustrations on *other* folks (parents, textbook publishers, educators, bike thieves).

Change is always hard. But the degree of difficulty depends on a measure's complexity, how much local support it has, and how thoroughly it's been thought through. These are all things over which reformers have a lot of control. The further away from communities and families a policy is written, and the more moving parts it has, the more likely it is to encounter trouble.

In response, there's a tendency to insist that the policy is sound and any issues are just "implementation problems." I'll put this bluntly: there's no such thing as an implementation problem. What matters in schooling is what actually happens to 50 million kids in 100,000 schools. That's *all* implementation. Calling something an implementation problem is how we reformers let ourselves off the hook. It's a fancy way to avoid saying that we didn't realize how a new policy would affect real people . . . and that it turned out worse than promised. The proper word for that is *problem*. Period. Responsible reformers take pride in crafting policies that work in reality like they do in theory and then own the results if they don't. I hope you'll hold yourself to that standard. It's a good one.

5

Why You Shouldn't
Put Too Much
Faith in Experts

DO YOU KNOW THE STORY of Paul the Octopus? During the 2008 Euro soccer tournament, Paul was tasked by his caretakers at Sea Life Oberhausen with picking the winner of each German match. They'd hold up two glass boxes, each marked with a team's flag, and Paul would pick one. By the time the 2010 World Cup rolled around, Paul had rounded into fine form. He correctly predicted the winner in each of Germany's games and the championship match, racking up a sterling 8-0 record—the odds against that were 256 to 1![1]

Paul's blind guesses turned out to be a whole lot better than most of the experts' picks. This phenomenon is far more common than you might expect. Three-quarters or more of "expert" mutual fund managers, for instance, even with all their experience and high-powered analytics, do *worse* than the stock market average.[2] More often than not, this means that you'd be better off letting an octopus pick your stocks than having a stock market expert do so.

That brings us to the larger point, which is how reformers should think about expertise. Back when today's big-R reformers were on the outside looking in, they evinced a healthy skepticism of expertise. But, when they began to occupy positions of power and get hailed as experts, they developed a newfound respect for it. Not surprisingly, it turns out that expertise is much more compelling when we agree with the advice.

I've gone the other way. Once upon a time, I thought that experts were people who understood the world better than the rest of us. Nowadays, I think that they're people who know a lot about particular things, and that their narrow expertise is not always helpful.

Don't get me wrong. I'm a huge fan of expertise when it involves using specific mastery to perform a specific task. I'm very happy to defer to cardiovascular surgeons, electricians, or speech pathologists when it comes to their specialty.

When talking about broad reforms to health care, energy policy, or education, however, it's a different story. I've found that experts often forget that their expertise represents just a tiny sliver of the world, and thus overestimate how much they know and what it can tell us. And that can cause problems.

As a kid, I revered expertise. When I was a teen, my dad promised me that, if I gave my old bike to my little brother, I could have his beat-up Honda Civic. The catch was that the Civic no longer ran. My dad (a pretty fair bootstrap mechanic) and I were going to fix it. I recall the Saturday we popped the hood to reveal an indecipherable spaghetti bowl of hoses, molded steel, and wiring. One thought ran through my mind: "No way." I felt like I could have studied that engine for a month and it wouldn't help.

There's no happy redemption story here, no triumphant tale of the "growth mind-set." I threw in the towel and bought an old Plymouth Duster for $900. I remember the incident because it captures how totally perplexing I always found the world.

As a high schooler and college student, when I read about new technologies, social policies, or arms control negotiations, I was intimidated just thinking about how much the people doing this stuff must know and how smart they must be. I'd sometimes wonder where these experts even came from.

As a college senior, I recall waiting to take the GRE in political science. Listening to the confident chatter of the students around me, I was filled with self-doubt. The room seemed full of budding experts. I wondered how they could know so much and how I would ever keep up.

Imagine my surprise when my GRE scores arrived and I realized I must have outperformed just about everyone in that room. When I was admitted to the doctoral program in politics at Harvard, I was once again daunted by the smarts, drive, and worldliness of my colleagues. But I did just fine.

When I finished graduate school, I managed to land at the University of Virginia. I started to publish books, give speeches, and get quoted by journalists. Along the way, I'd begun to notice that the experts I encountered weren't obviously smarter or more knowledgeable than I was. Indeed, I soon realized that I had somehow *become* one of the "experts." This was a problem, because I wasn't sure that I had much more business offering wisdom on American schools than I did trying to fix a car. In the immortal words of Scooby Doo, "Ruh roh!".

I figured there were only two explanations for my newfound status. One was that I was a poseur who would be found out in due time. The second was that I was actually an expert. If it was the second, though, I thought that most of my peers should be much more modest about their expertise, too.

Over two decades, I've become convinced that the second explanation is (probably) the right one. Expertise tends to be a lot less expert than people think. I can't tell you how many times I've met a renowned superintendent or researcher and wondered why her pedantic pronouncements are treated breathlessly when other superintendents or researchers say similar things and get only shrugs. I've grown to suspect that a lot of reform expertise may be mostly a matter of self-promotion, boundless self-confidence, and being in the right place at the right time.

All this applies to me as well, obviously. When asked to give talks, write articles, or advise educators and public officials, the truth is that I'm frequently repeating ideas and suggestions that my audience has heard before. Because I'm an "expert," though, my words carry extra weight. And while I've written lots of books and done lots of workshops offering my best advice, I'd be lying if I told you that I know what I'm saying is "right."

That's the point, really. It's not that expertise is irrelevant. I do know some things and I like to think I have some wisdom to offer. But expertise is much fuzzier and more limited than people typically recognize, especially when the talk turns to "listening to the experts" or "deferring to expertise."

The problem is less with expertise itself than with what it can do to our judgment. Economist Noreena Hertz explains, "We've become addicted to experts. We've become addicted to their certainty, their assuredness, their definitiveness, and in the process, we have ceded our responsibility." Hertz, author of *Eyes Wide Open: How to Make Smart Decisions in a Confusing World*, tells of an experiment in which participants received an MRI scan while making investment decisions. When investors were asked to think for themselves, their brains employed the circuits that calculate potential gains and weigh risk.

However, Hertz observes, when "they listened to . . . experts' voices, the independent decision-making parts of their brains switched off. [They] literally flat-lined." The subjects outsourced the work their brains would normally have done.[3] As the *Wall Street Journal*'s Jason Zweig puts it, the "circuits stayed quiet even when the expert's advice was bad . . . In the presence of a financial adviser, your brain can empty out like a dump truck."[4] Gregory Berns of Emory University, a coauthor of the study, observes, "People have this tendency to turn off their own capacity for making judgments when an expert comes into the picture."[5]

And we need our judgment turned on, because expertise should be consumed with care. In pretty much any realm where experts are asked to make predictions, the results leave a lot to be desired. Professional talent evaluators have a famously uneven track record in the NFL, NBA, and major league baseball drafts. Industry executives have a horrendous record of predicting which movies or television shows will be hits. And then there's publishing, with countless examples of best-sellers and classics getting repeatedly rejected. Just think of J.K. Rowling's first Harry Potter book (*Harry Potter and the Sorcerer's Stone*), which was turned down a dozen times in the United Kingdom, or *The Tale of Peter Rabbit*, which author Beatrix Potter had to self-publish after a parade of rejection slips.[6]

In his book *Expert Political Judgment*, University of Pennsylvania professor Philip Tetlock asked 284 political and economic experts to make thousands of predictions over an extended period of time. In each case, he asked whether they expected the status quo, more of x, or less of x. The result? As journalist Louis Menand put it, "The experts performed worse than they would have if they had simply assigned an equal probability to all three outcomes . . . Human beings who spend their lives studying the state of the world, in other words, are poorer forecasters than dart-throwing monkeys."[7] You'll notice a theme here.

All that said, it's worth repeating: expertise *is* real. Dentists are experts at drilling teeth, welders at welding parts, and psychometricians at designing test questions. When you ask experts to do precise tasks in which they have particular training, you'll be much better off than if you ask a non-expert. The confusion is when we think that specialized knowledge will make someone expert about complex efforts that stretch far beyond their technical mastery.

Wedded to what they think they know and expect to see, experts are handicapped when anticipating change or dealing with real-world complications. They tend to become myopic, trapped in thought bubbles of their own making. This happens because, if you have one good idea, there are huge rewards for spending a career saying it in increasingly elaborate forms.

Academics known for their one big idea get hired by prestigious universities and can spend decades tacking fine print onto it. Consultants deemed "expert" on a policy or program can earn tidy sums giving variations on the same advice to a series of school districts or foundations.

Experts naturally wind up in love with the ideas, approaches, or experiences that made them successful. That love gets passed onto their admirers and acolytes. One result is that expertise tends to stifle alternative perspectives, with really influential experts smothering dissent and promoting groupthink.

Invited to address friendly audiences, linked with like-minded peers, and celebrated by adoring disciples, experts wind up cloistered. It's surprisingly easy for a guru to go long stretches without really having to engage dissenting views or answer for disappointing results. Thus, when experts do opine on broad questions, their solutions to complex problems of policy and practice can prove to be parochial, shortsighted, and naive.

Experts also tend to be remarkably unaccountable. Once you've been labeled an expert, there are few consequences for being wrong. You can be wrong time and again and never get called on it. This applies in politics, policy, sports, finance . . . and also in schooling. Education experts can offer lousy advice or unworkable stratagems and then wave off the consequences as "implementation problems" or simply as evidence that what they're trying to do is really difficult.

So what should a reformer make of all this?

For one thing, be appropriately skeptical when an expert declares that "these are the best reading programs, school systems, or researchers." We ought to be much humbler about such claims. When reporters or headhunters call me and ask which school districts are doing great work, I don't have any objective way to judge—so my "expertise" is largely a matter of naming a superintendent I like or find impressive. Whether they'll admit it or not, that's true of most experts.

For another, recognize that the impulse to defer to expertise can rob us of perspective and cloud our judgment. When it comes to system change, expertise may only apply to a tiny sliver of what's involved. It's usually a mistake to defer to experts on anything that extends beyond that sliver. Expertise in the mechanics of site-based governance, for instance, can yield blind enthusiasm for state policies mandating new site-based governance councils, even if those are ill conceived or poorly designed. Worse, the tendency to defer to experts can shortchange common sense or make nonexperts fearful of asking simple questions like, "Umm, will this work?"

As long as we respect its limits, of course, expertise has great value—especially when it comes to tasks that are discrete, concrete, and specialized. So, I'm decidedly not suggesting education reformers should reject expertise. I *am* saying that they should treat it with sensible skepticism. After all, it was President Herbert Hoover who declared in his 1929 inaugural address, mere months before the start of the Great Depression, "In no nation are the fruits of accomplishment more secure."[8] It was Thomas Watson, the chairman of IBM, who predicted in 1943, "I think there is a world market for maybe five computers."[9] And it was Admiral William Leahy who said during World War II, "The [atomic] bomb will never go off. I speak as an expert in explosives."[10]

Speaking as an expert, I can tell you that expertise isn't always all it's cracked up to be.

6

A Letter to a Younger Me

PENNING THESE LETTERS has loosened a bunch of memories. Lots of them, I'm afraid, have me wondering what the hell I was thinking. I'm going to share some things I wish I could have told a younger me in the hope that you might find them useful.

Young Rick—this all feels very *Bill and Ted's Excellent Adventure*, especially the moment when they go back in time so Ted can remind younger Ted to set his watch—young Rick, be careful what you wish for. You're going to spend years arguing that Washington has a vital role to play in promoting educational transparency. You're going to contend that regular, comparable test results are a good way to inform educators, families, and communities, and can serve as an alternative to Washington decrees on how to evaluate or intervene in schools. Then reality will slap you around. Transparency will morph into an excuse for enthusiastic federal bureaucrats, overcaffeinated lawyers, and big-R Reformers to issue new directives and demand new laws. Basically, all the stuff you think is unhelpful.

Don't take it personally and don't make it personal. You didn't get into this to make enemies or pick fights. But in school reform, when people dislike an idea or an argument, some will make it all about you. You're going to hear, usually secondhand, that this or that colleague said you didn't know your ass from your elbow. Your big-R Reform friends are going to deride you when you stray too far from their program. Shake it off. It can feel personal, but it's really not. It's about honest, important disagreements. You'll fare best when you keep your cool. Frustration can cause you to forget that and lash out, but doing so is almost always self-defeating.

Here's what I mean. You and I have always opposed race-based affirmative action. Especially in school reform circles, many see such a view as misguided, ignorant, or bigoted—and they sometimes say so in pointed terms. Recall the woman who told you at a panel event, "Sounds to me like you just don't want blacks to go to college." While you fumbled for a response, she added, "I guess you figure those black kids can always take classes in prison." I can't remember what you said, only that it was flustered, defensive, and incoherent. That achieved nothing and gave onlookers no reason to grant you the benefit of the doubt.

Nowadays, when I've kept my cool, people have frequently said that—even when they disagree—my remarks helped them make sense of my views. I recall talking to a group of teachers in Chicago where one asked if I agreed with "deformers" that districts should fire more teachers. I said, "Yep." That prompted a wave of eye rolling and angry comments. I kept it together and said, "Look, *teachers* say that 5 percent of the teachers in their school deserve an 'F.' The average Fortune 500 firm fires 1 to 2 percent of employees a year. But districts are firing a tiny fraction of 1 percent of teachers. I think that should probably be closer to 2 percent." I don't know if I swayed anybody, but the discussion wound up being civil and constructive. And, if the chatter afterward was an indication, at least a few teachers were reflecting on what I'd said. Rick, remember that you're doing this work because you believe it's important; others are, too. There's opportunity for insight and understanding if you seize it.

It's okay to admit what you don't know. Screenwriter William Goldman famously said of Hollywood, "Nobody knows anything." His point? For all the slick analyses, industry jargon, and staggering salaries, nobody in Hollywood really knows why some movies succeed and some don't. I've found that Goldman's wisdom applies equally well to school reform. People will tell you why this district should be a national model or that superintendent is a genius. Most of the time, I've discovered, they don't really know what they're talking about. They were impressed by a big speech, read a study, are repeating what somebody told them, or were dazzled by a nifty school tour. It's tempting to do the same, especially when it gets you on TV or quoted in the newspapers. But try to resist.

In fact, do me a favor and learn to hush up. I recall a mentor seeing me eyeball the clock during one endless meeting. "We're not done yet," he murmured. "Everything's been said, but everyone hasn't said it." I've fallen into that trap as much as anyone. It's natural to want people to know that you've got something to say. But there's a lot of clutter out there. When you don't have anything useful to add, it's okay to be quiet.

Be gentle with yourself and with your colleagues. When you get frustrated and indignant, take a deep breath. When you're at the University of Virginia, you're going to invest way too much energy running a monthly speaker series that attracts maybe three dozen people. You're going to drive yourself crazy over schedules and attendance. You're going to annoy colleagues who have more perspective. Getting agitated doesn't make an event more valuable or help it run more smoothly. Exhale. Then just do the best you can.

It's surprising how readily good ideas can morph into bad ones. In a few years, one of your friends, a guy credited with helping to invent "No Excuses" charter schools, will lament that he wishes he could put that genie back in the bottle. Why? He fears the "No Excuses" mentality is encouraging a lot of tough talk and dumb decisions. He'll note that his school's *actual* mantra had been "No Shortcuts"—teaching kids to take pride in their work and finish what they started. He'll tell you, "We never talked about 'No Excuses.' In fact, our credo was: 'If there's a problem, we look for a solution. If there's a better way, we find it. If a teammate needs help, we give it. If we need help, we ask.' So there were always plenty of excuses; the question was how to deal with them." He'll sigh, "'No Excuses' sounds close to 'No Shortcuts,' but I guess I should've been more aggressive in policing the T-shirts." Good ideas can mutate in ways you don't anticipate.

Judge people for yourself. It can be easy to inherit likes and dislikes from allies and mentors, to start thinking that "these" people are on my side and "those" aren't. You think, "Since my side is full of smart, caring people, those on the other side must be mean-spirited hacks." Remember one of your first school choice conclaves, when the convener kicked things off by saying, "It's wonderful to be among so many impassioned warriors for children. We've got the angels with us right here"? Do you remember wondering if you were in the wrong room, since you didn't feel much like either a warrior or an angel? The convener said, "We're going to beat the unions, with all their money and their goons." These days, I know that just about any gathering can sound like this (though the identity of the angels and the goons will vary depending on the host), but I keep meeting supposedly awful people and finding them decent and reasonable. Make it a point to meet people on the "other side" and judge them for yourself.

Spend less time thinking up ways to spend new education dollars and more about how to spend the money that's already there. After your first year of teaching, you'll chat with your old economics professor. At one point, he'll ask, "Rick, out of curiosity, what would you do if someone doubled your school's budget?" "There's so much!" you'll babble. "I'd raise teacher pay by 50 percent. I'd get new textbooks and copiers. I'd hire two more counselors . . . " He'll listen for a while and then ask why you're so sure that the money will be well spent. You'll hem and haw. He'll ask if any spending could sensibly be cut. You won't have an answer. The funny thing is, he's a liberal who teaches the economics of education and supports more school spending—and you *still* won't be able to sell him! That's because you won't know what problem you're trying to solve or what the money is supposed to do. Money can seem like the easiest answer to any problem, but its value always depends on how well and wisely it's used.

Don't spend too much time sweating those who truly, fundamentally disagree with you. If they've thought things through and see them differently, that's their prerogative. Focus instead on swaying those who are less sure or less informed. In football terms, policy debates are mostly won between the forty-yard lines. This means you usually win by appealing to moderates, undecideds, and people with other things on their mind, not by converting those who think you're flat wrong. If you can get 60 percent of people to agree with you, you're going to win most of the time. This also means you want your agenda to seem relevant and helpful to those between the forties and not just to those who are already with you.

Steer clear of words that have been stripped of meaning. School reform is filled with such words: *consensus, best practices, differentiation, twenty-first-century skills, rigor, effective teaching, accountability, empowerment,* and many more. Most of the time, it's not clear what any of these place-holders really mean. Truth is, they're often used to avoid inconvenient or uncomfortable precision. The problem is that mushy language leads to fuzzy thinking. When I use these words, I frequently realize that even *I* don't know exactly what I'm saying. Try to avoid spewing word salad, and talk instead in terms of actions, specifics, and proper nouns.

Choices always have a price. Only want a job where you can speak your mind? That's cool. Just know that there are places you won't go, opportunities you won't get, and meetings you won't be invited to unless you're a team player. You're going to write and say stuff that annoys your friends at big foundations and at the US Department of Education, and it's going to cost you dollars, access, and even friendships. That stinks, but it's how the world works. Do your best to think your choices through before you speak or act. That way, when the bill comes due, you won't be surprised or disappointed.

Remember that the phrase "getting to scale" can be a trap. Since the goal of reform is to do good things for more kids, those words tend to create the impression that the "real" action is in sweeping policy change. That will tempt you to downplay or pooh-pooh promising reforms that help some kids, because they *only* help some kids. The pursuit of scale can also be a recipe for turning small successes into grim, sprawling failures. Know that some things scale naturally and others don't. Technological solutions scale more readily than those dependent on exquisite skill. Apps that help teachers manage classrooms or parents assist students with homework are simple to use and can be offered to four million users as readily as to four hundred. So, if you want to pursue scale by designing educational software, knock yourself out. But much of what you're thinking about when you say "scale" usually involves trying to get huge numbers of schools and districts to do complicated things a certain way. So long as that's your goal, scale is going to require immense patience and heaps of humility. Make your peace with that.

It's a long, winding journey. Try not to get too high or too low, because it all evens out over time. You're going to spend three weeks in the Republic of Georgia (the country on the Black Sea, not the state with the Coca-Cola museum) advising the Ministry of Education. For the first week, you're going to visit schools, traveling from Tbilisi to the Black Sea in an oversized SUV. You'll be accompanied by your pistol-packing driver, a translator with suspect English, a government liaison with more than a passing resemblance to Stalin, and an enormous "chief of party." You'll make an obligatory stop at the Stalin museum and pass within a few miles of the encamped Russian army. You'll visit three or four worn, depressing schools a day. The visits will consist of stilted conversations with nervous principals who share ceremonial bowls of cherries while carefully saying nothing that could get them in trouble.

The hotels will be dubious, especially the one where your oversized chief of party falls through his shower (his fall happily broken by the subflooring—you've got to love Soviet architecture). You'll be lonely, exhausted, and frustrated. You'll wonder what the hell you're doing over there, doubt you're adding any value, and start to think the whole thing was a big mistake. But you know what? You'll eventually make it to the shore of the Black Sea, and it'll all be okay. You'll have fish and beer, laugh about the journey in suspect English, and provide the ministry with a few thoughts that might prove helpful. Things are never as bad or as good as they seem. Tough stretches can seem like they'll never end. But they do. So be patient, be of good cheer, and gird yourself for the long haul.

I know you'll have to learn most of this the hard way. Such is life. But please do me one little favor: say "yes" when you can. It'll lead you to all sorts of interesting places.

7

The Handshake Between Families and Schools

THE CONVICTION THAT EVERY CHILD can succeed wasn't always the norm in schooling. Over the past two decades, however, reformers have spent enormous time and energy insisting that educators be responsible for educating every child. Today, we largely take that mission for granted. That represents a tectonic shift—and a tremendous, important victory.

Back in the 1980s and 1990s, American education paid a lot of attention to the quality of parenting and far too little to the quality of teaching and schooling. Complaints that parents weren't doing their part too often seemed to be an excuse for lousy schools. It wasn't unusual to hear educators declare that certain students were unteachable or that they shouldn't be blamed for not teaching kids who weren't there to learn.

When I think back on that era, there's one anecdote that inevitably comes to mind. In the mid-1990s, I supervised a half-dozen student teachers each semester for Harvard's Graduate School of Education. I'd visit a school, meet with the student teacher and his or her mentor teacher, observe a class, discuss what had gone down, and then write it up for the official file.

This memory concerns one visit to an iconic Boston high school. The place was old, beat-up, and known for mediocre results. The student teacher was working with a pleasant, world-weary mentor. Let's call them Jim and Mr. Mahoney.

The bell rang and Jim started the lesson. It was a social studies class. In a room of thirty or thirty-five kids, there were maybe a dozen in front who were taking notes, participating, and paying attention. The rest of the kids were passing notes, staring out the window, and generally tuning out. Jim tried moving around, calling on different kids, and using a small group activity to engage everyone, but none of it made much difference.

The class finally ended and the students shuffled out. The three of us sat down to talk. I asked Mr. Mahoney, "So, how'd you think the class went?"

He took his glasses off and polished them on his shirt as he said, "I thought it was terrific. Jim was organized. He changed things up. He worked hard. It was a really nice lesson." He paused, then said, "What really impressed me was how engaged the students were."

I wondered if he was kidding. He didn't seem to be. "Mm-hmm, that's really useful," I said. I paused. "Here's the thing. To me, it looked like maybe ten students were really involved, as you're saying, but also like a lot of kids weren't. Did I miss something? It sounds like you might've seen something I didn't."

What he said next has always stuck with me. He said, "No, that's about right. But Jim had all of the students who were here to learn. The others, the knuckleheads, well, you just want to keep them in line. And he did fine on that, too."

Today, that mind-set is considered unacceptable. If educators say such things, they'll usually mutter them privately. Teachers and schools are expected to teach every child. That's a wonderful thing.

I fear, though, that it's come at a cost. The insistence that kids and parents also need to do their part has been lost along the way. In this era of accountability, talk of parental responsibility has come to be seen as little more than a case of blaming the victim. Reformers worry that such talk can open the door to low expectations, or that it'll let schools and educators off the hook.

The result is that we just don't talk very much anymore about whether parents are pushing kids to do their homework or respect their teachers. Everyone agrees that it's swell if parents do, but it's just not polite to discuss it in public. When students are truant, reformers hesitate to say anything that would imply parents are at fault. When only a handful of parents show up at parent-teacher meetings—even after educators rearrange their schedules to accommodate them—reformers are conspicuously mum. If they do take note, it's usually only to lament that parents are overworked and overburdened.

When teachers get frustrated by any of this, reformers just shrug and tell them not to make excuses.

These are obviously sensitive, thorny questions. Parents frequently *are* overworked and overburdened. And I don't want to suggest that there are simple answers. But reformers would benefit from being more willing to talk about what we should expect of parents. There's a balance between families and schools, and we seem to have tipped from one extreme to the other.

Education is always a handshake between families and teachers, between students and schools. Compulsory attendance laws can make children show up, but it's incredibly hard to teach someone who doesn't want to learn. Now, it's entirely true that part of a teacher's job is finding the way to open a student's heart and mind. By the same token, though, the job of parents and guardians is to raise children who are responsible, respectful, and ready to learn.

It can help to think about this in terms of health care. When we say someone is a good doctor, we mean that they're competent and responsible; they diagnose your condition and suggest the right treatment. We don't mean that they perform miracles. If a doctor tells you to reduce your cholesterol and you keep eating steak, we don't blame the physician or label her a "bad doctor." We hold the doctor responsible for doing her job, but we expect patients to do their part, too. This is the implicit handshake between doctor and patient, and saying so isn't seen as "blaming" the patient.

When the patient is a child, the relationship is the same—though parents assume a crucial role. If a diabetic child ignores the doctor's instructions on monitoring blood sugar or administering insulin, we don't blame the doctor. And we don't blame the kid. We expect parents to take responsibility for learning what's required, doing it or else teaching the child to do it, and making sure it gets done.

When it comes to the handshake between parents and educators, though, that same understanding has broken down. Straight talk about parental responsibility is greeted with resistance, criticism, and even accusations of racism. Few have the inclination, credibility, and platform to address this effectively. That's a problem because there's much worth saying.

Barack Obama wasn't my favorite president, but one of the things I admired about him was his willingness to address this challenge. In 2014, speaking about his "My Brother's Keeper" initiative, Obama said:

> We can help give every child access to quality preschool and help them start learning from an early age, but we can't replace the power of a parent who's reading to that child. We can reform our criminal justice system to ensure that it's not infected with bias, but nothing keeps a young man out of trouble like a father who takes an active role in his son's life. In other words, broadening the horizons for our young men and giving them the tools they need to succeed will require a sustained effort from all of us. Parents will have to parent—and turn off the television, and help with homework.[1]

Not everyone is Obama. As the first black president, as a child raised by a single mother, and as an esteemed father, he was uniquely positioned to say these things. But those sentiments are crucial and should be repeated often.

We should expect *all* parents, of every race and creed, to do their best to clasp hands with their children's teachers. That was Obama's essential point, and it's one where we should be able to find common ground. After all, parents have an outsized impact on their children's academic future. Children whose parents read to them, talk to them, and teach them patience and self-discipline are more likely to succeed academically. Parenting influences everything from how much TV kids watch to whether they show up to school.

The point is decidedly *not* to scapegoat parents or to judge them. Parenthood is hard work, and I'm no better at it than anyone else. I've stood wooden while my son Gray face-planted off our front steps or his chair. I've caved when he or his brother refused to finish their dinner or brush their teeth. I've shouted in frustration when they've thrown food or tantrums. I've let them watch hour upon hour of inane truck videos, fed them junk, and spoiled them when I didn't have the energy to rein them in. Given my own manifest limitations, I have zero interest in sounding self-righteous or pretending to have the answers. My point is that we need to be frank about what that handshake between families and schools requires, clarify for parents what they should be doing, and help them do those things well.

Here's what I have in mind. I once visited with the director of an urban literacy program. He talked to me about why some parents don't read to their kids, or why their reading doesn't help as much as it should.

"Rick," he said, "the stuff we take for granted would really blow your mind. I remember this one father. He was a high school dropout and working a tough job, but he was doing what we tell them. He was making the time. He had his infant on his lap and was reading. But he didn't have that picture of 'reading to a kid' that you and I take for granted."

"How do you mean?" I asked.

"He was reading, but it wasn't what we usually think of as reading to an infant. It was like he was reading the paper. He wasn't varying his voice or using inflection. He wasn't pointing to pictures. He was intent on reading every word before turning the page. He had the kid planted awkwardly on his knee, and neither of them looked comfortable."

He said, "We worked with the dad on all that. Showed him how to position the kid more comfortably. Had him point out pictures, change up his voice, and have more fun with it. That's all it really took. The next month, it was a different story."

When asking parents to clasp hands with educators, things like support, expectations, and peer pressure can make a huge difference. Reformers need to think not just about how schools and teachers can do better but also about what it means for parents to do better. In both cases, change is partly a matter of appreciation and problem solving—and partly a matter of tough love.

This isn't an either-or. Everyone needs to step up.

None of this is new. Thousands of years ago, the Greeks wrestled with how to balance the educational responsibilities of the family and the state. Plato famously suggested eliminating parents from the childrearing equation so that the state could properly raise its future leaders and guardians. In other words, he thought parenting was too important to be left to parents. That's not the path we've chosen, thank heavens.

Today, we've come a long way from Mr. Mahoney's world. We ask educators to be responsible for the success of all their students. That's an unequivocally good thing. How students fare, though, is also a product of whether they study at home and take their schoolwork seriously. Some of that truly is beyond the reach of educators.

When reformers hesitate to address the role of parents and families, they can give educators the impression that they're more interested in finding scapegoats than in improving schools. When reformers do speak to parents as well as educators, they forge trust with teachers, help parents do the right thing, and foster the kind of school communities that lead to lasting success. So, by all means, call schools and educators to account—just do it for parents, too.

8

The Thing About Data

THE FIRST TIME I HEARD of Campbell's Law was in a college class in public policy. The professor asked, "Can data can ever cause problems? Can it ever hurt?" It seemed like a trick question. We puzzled over it. When he called on us, we all uncertainly shook our heads or mumbled a version of "I don't think so."

He asked, "What if a police department decides to evaluate officers based on the number of traffic tickets they write? Could anything go wrong?" Someone pointed out the obvious, that cops would try to write lots of tickets—including for people who might not deserve them. And that might come at the expense of something more important.

The professor said, "What if the same department decides that it wants to make sure the officers don't neglect their patrols, so it also gives credit for making more arrests?" This time a couple of students observed that officers might make arrests even when a less drastic response was called for.

He asked, "Okay, so what if they flip it? What if they reward cops who have fewer arrests and reported disturbances?" Well, duh. Police might turn a blind eye to real problems.

The instructor smiled and said, "See? You can think of lots of ways where data might hurt." With that, he introduced us to Campbell's Law. Formulated in 1976 by social psychologist Donald Campbell, it reads, "The more any quantitative social indicator is used for social decision-making, the more subject it will be to corruption pressures and the more apt it will be to distort and corrupt the social processes it is intended to monitor."[1]

One student said, "But you're not showing that the data itself actually hurts. These are all examples of where it's only a problem if you use it in dumb ways." She was right, of course. Data itself can't usually hurt you (unless a stack of printouts falls on your foot), but it does turn out to be remarkably easy to use data in destructive ways.

Campbell's Law may be the single most important thing to keep in mind when talking about metrics, the power of data, and data-driven decisions. If it helps, a simpler way to restate it is: "When a measure becomes a target, it ceases to be a good measure."

When you put a lot of weight on a given measure, people react. When they do, it can mess up the measure and create incentives you never anticipated. What at first seems like a smart, clever, and cutting-edge way to use data can look very different in hindsight.

This happens in all walks of life. In 1999, a flight from New York to Seattle took 22 minutes and 48 seconds longer than it had a decade earlier—even though planes were more sophisticated and stayed in the air for the same amount of time. What had happened? In the interim, Washington had started reporting airline "on-time arrival rates." Airlines responded by boarding earlier and pushing back expected arrival times to make it easier for flights to be reported as "on time." So passengers spent more time sitting on the tarmac. That emphasis on "timeliness" lengthened scheduled travel time by 130 million minutes between 1989 and 1999.[2] Whoops.

The former Soviet Union was something of a case study in Campbell's Law, with factories under the gun to meet arbitrary government production targets. Factory directors were judged on whether they hit their targets, rather than on efficiency, customer satisfaction, or product quality. When five-year plans set targets in terms of tonnage, factories made things that were comically heavy. This yielded chandeliers that pulled down ceilings, and roofing metal that collapsed the buildings on which it sat. At other times, auto factories hit their quotas by manufacturing cars without key components—like engines.[3]

Sometimes the workings of Campbell's Law can get downright gruesome. During the Vietnam War, US Army combat units were evaluated on the number of enemy soldiers killed. This encouraged them to maximize kills. Sociologist Tony Waters has noted, "This measure was corrupted as dead civilians were re-defined as 'enemy,' and occasionally villages were invaded" to boost the number of enemy casualties.[4] Even beyond the head-shaking amorality at work, the metric led soldiers to act in ways that probably hurt the war effort.

In education, reformers have frequently been blindsided by Campbell's Law. Big-*R* Reformers have been intent on evaluating schools and teachers using a few simple metrics, primarily reading and math scores. This has given educators cause to do everything possible to boost those results—to the point that it can bring to mind those old Soviet factories. Schools have embraced practice tests and test preparation. They've given students more reading and math instruction, and less science and history. All of this means that test results can improve even if students aren't actually learning more.

Campbell's Law applies to a lot more than test scores, of course. The No Child Left Behind Act stipulated that school violence be tracked in order to identify "persistently dangerous" schools. What happened? In hundreds of districts, reported incidents of school violence dropped nearly to zero. Had schools suddenly become much safer? Nah. A lot of schools just stopped reporting incidents.

As I write, reformers are pushing to incorporate measures of "social and emotional learning" into state accountability systems. These measures, of things like persistence and growth mind-set, are good and useful (as are reading and math scores and data on school violence). But recognize that turning them into formal measures will give educators incentive to do anything they can to juice the reported outcomes—even if the strategies are silly, boring, or a waste of class time.

I can hear you thinking, "But we *want* kids to know reading and math and we *want* them to be persistent. Are you saying we shouldn't measure these things?"

Not at all. But here's the thing: there can be a big difference between knowing math and doing well on a math test, or being persistent and doing well on a persistence assessment (just as there is between making cars and making cars *with* engines). When the stakes are low, the difference between these tends to be pretty small. When results start to matter, though, the pressure can yield deceptive or misleading results. That does *not* mean we shouldn't test or measure, but it *does* mean we need to be conscientious about how we test and what we measure.

I've been at this long enough to watch American education do a 180 on this question. In the 1990s, it was frighteningly easy to find education leaders who were dismissive of outcome measures. Today, big-*R* Reformers champion them. That's good. I fear, though, that they've learned the lyrics and not the music. If ignoring data and metrics was "the old stupid," the slapdash embrace of half-baked data is "the new stupid."

This first struck me several years ago, while talking to a group of young leaders training to be superintendents. They were accomplished, passionate, and eager to make a difference. At one point, we wound up discussing value-added assessment and how to use it.

The group had recently read a research brief noting that, in any given district, teachers with higher value-added scores seem to cluster in higher-income, higher-performing schools. To enthusiastic nods, one young leader declared, "Day one, we're going to start identifying those high value-added teachers and moving them to the schools that really need them."

Curious how much they'd thought this through, I asked a bunch of questions: How much faith did they have in value-added measures as a reliable gauge of performance? How confident were they that teachers effective in one school would be equally effective in a new school? How concerned were they that this might cause some teachers to depart? How would they get teachers to embrace their new assignments? How did they know which schools "really needed" good teachers?

I didn't mind the lack of firm answers to these questions. What made me uneasy was the sense that they regarded such questions as distractions. One woman captured the vibe when she impatiently declared, "We need to act. We've got children who need help, and we know which teachers can help them." Right then, I glumly envisioned a new generation of superintendents shuffling teachers between schools, getting frustrated at the disappointing results, lamenting an unexpected exodus of terrific teachers, and wondering what had gone wrong.

Data is a tool. Even flawed data can be helpful. But what matters is what you do with it. Data is most useful when you're using it to inform decisions rather than asking it to make decisions for you. It's absolutely fine for leaders to use value-added when thinking about teacher assignment. But those scores shouldn't be treated as sacrosanct and they certainly shouldn't be permitted to dictate staffing policy. Rather, leaders should use those results as an excuse to ask questions about how transferable classroom performance really is, how and when to relocate teachers, what will keep teachers from leaving, and more.

"Moneyball" provides a nice illustration of what I'm talking about. The term derives from the title of Michael Lewis's intriguing book, which examined how Oakland A's general manager Billy Beane managed to field consistently terrific baseball teams in the early aughts even as his penny-pinching franchise spent a lot less than most teams. Lewis explains that the A's used sophisticated statistical analysis to identify overlooked talent and to determine which strategies they should employ. As a result, they dramatically outperformed expectations.[5]

Naturally, this fueled a wave of imitators across baseball and, eventually, other professional sports. School reformers learned about all this and wisely figured that the same kinds of tools could help spur school improvement. So far, so good.

Here's the thing, though. The problem prior to Beane's revolution in Oakland was not an absence of data. In fact, baseball has been a geek haven for generations *because* of all its statistics. The problem was that the most commonly used stats—home runs, runs batted in, batting average, and so on—are flawed measures of individual performance. They're massively incomplete. They routinely misstate a player's value by ignoring things like the stadium he plays in or how often his teammates get on base. As a result, when teams looked at those stats, they'd overpay for some players and overlook others. The new metrics helped Beane find players whose talents were slighted by the traditional statistics. They allowed him to build terrific teams at bargain basement prices.

Today's math and reading scores, value-added metrics, and gauges of social and emotional learning are *not* an example of playing moneyball.

They mean, rather, that education has finally caught up to baseball's *pre-moneyball* era. That's a big improvement from where schooling used to be, but let's not get ahead of ourselves. While helpful, these data are primitive, limited, and often misleading. Education's moneyball moment awaits the collection of deep, systematic data on the processes of teaching, learning, and school operations.

Here's what I mean: Reading and math scores are really useful for parents and policymakers who want a snapshot of how students and schools are doing. At the same time, knowing that this school tested much better than that school doesn't say much about why that was so or about how to help either school improve. What *does* help on that count is breaking down what happens in classrooms: tracking how class time is utilized, which textbooks are being read, or how frequently teachers use formative assessments. These moneyball-style metrics are crucial for improvement but have been overlooked amidst our fascination with testing.

These days, people routinely say "effective teachers" when they mean "teachers who have high value-added scores in reading and math." People say a school is doing a great job when they mean "it has really high scores in reading and math." But reading and math are only a slice of what schools are supposed to teach, and it's not clear how fully our tests reflect mastery even in those domains. Using these scores as a proxy for overall quality is especially awkward because there's remarkably little evidence that they tell us much about other things we care about, like college-going, employment, citizenship, or creativity.

I've found one simple question that seems to provoke useful discussion about all this: "What percentage of what you want schools to do is reflected in reading and math scores?" For me, the answer is about 30 or 35 percent. Interestingly, many reformers give similar answers, even ones who talk about what "works" almost entirely in terms of reading and math scores.

Test scores measure something real and important. We shouldn't shy away from using them. But we also shouldn't overuse them or overstate their value. And, unless you think that reading and math scores capture the lion's share of what you want children to learn, you should be careful not to treat them as simple proxies for good schooling or teaching.

Metrics are a good and useful tool. And tools matter. Without tools, a carpenter is just a guy looking at a pile of wood. But even with the ultimate set of tools, a clumsy carpenter may do more harm than good—knocking holes in the wall and shorting out your electricity. What makes a good carpenter is not the tools; it's what he does with them. Remember that.

9

The Temptations
of Bureaucracy

THE WHO ONCE SANG, "Meet the new boss, same as the old boss."

In the early years of the Obama presidency, that old lyric kept coming to mind unbidden. This was back in 2009, when Congress created the $4.35 billion Race to the Top program as part of a $900 billion federal stimulus bill. Obama's Department of Education proceeded to use Race to the Top to get states to write five-hundred-page grant applications promising to adopt the department's preferred teacher evaluation policies, sign onto the Common Core, and do a bunch of other stuff on a nineteen-item checklist.

The irony was that many of the folks in charge had—until about five minutes earlier—been eloquent in explaining how bureaucracy stymied school reform. As entrepreneurs and advocates, they had prided themselves on their opposition to red tape and commitment to entrepreneurial rethinking. I knew them and knew they were sincere in all this.

Yet the moment they got the opportunity, they set aside their own work to join the federal bureaucracy. As one told me, "When your buddies go off to war, you go with them."

Big-R Reformers have come to imagine that going to Washington, giving speeches, issuing directives, and writing policies is the way to make meaningful change. This, they've seemingly decided, is how one makes a difference "at scale." Thus, once in office, they naturally threw themselves into the work of devising elaborate Washington-based plans. It was true that they'd always thought government micromanagement and bureaucracy were problems when done clumsily by the wrong people. But this was totally different. *This* was the *right* people doing it for the *right* reasons, and they thought that made all the difference. And they guilelessly rationalized all of it, taking umbrage at any suggestion that their handiwork might be producing red tape or stifling entrepreneurial rethinking.

I have a clear memory of one Washington dinner that a wealthy school reformer hosted in 2009. As the guests milled about before taking our seats, one of Obama's senior education people pushed over to me and said, more or less, "What is *wrong* with you, dude?"

You don't usually get this at a Washington dinner. People generally play it cool. Plus the guy was something of a friend. Taken aback, I cleverly responded, "Uh, what?"

He lit into me for being so critical of Race to the Top. He told me that I was just making trouble and trying to get attention. He said that, if I had suggestions, I could quietly, constructively pass them along. He said, "People in that office are busting their asses to do the right thing for kids, and you're just making it harder."

That kind of stuff drives me nuts. I said there were at least three things wrong with his analysis. One, I wasn't sure that Race to the Top would, in fact, be good for kids. Two, in America, when we disagree with what public officials are doing, we speak up. Three, I'd seen zero evidence that anyone in the Department of Education was inclined to listen to concerns or to discuss them.

He rolled his eyes. "What bulls#*t. You're stabbing us in the back while we're trying to jump-start state reform. We're getting states moving on school turnarounds, teacher evaluation, data . . . these are things you used to be for."

I said, "I'm still for them. But I don't think marching orders from Washington are the way to do them. You guys are telling states to make paper promises in order to get the money. This is stuff they'll do poorly or half-heartedly. I've never been for that."

Bristling, he brushed this aside, shook his finger at me, and said, "You need to decide whose side you're on."

I didn't have a response. In retrospect, I should have said, "You know whose side I'm *not* on? I'm not on the side of the self-assured bureaucrats who think they can fix schools from Washington. And you weren't on that side either, until you went to Washington and became a self-assured bureaucrat."

In fact, I should have had that response ready, because conversions of convenience are hardly uncommon. While serving as Chicago's superintendent, Obama's Secretary of Education Arne Duncan had declared No Child Left Behind a "broken" law. He said Washington needed to back off and let those closer to schools do their job. By the end of his tenure in Washington, he was battling to retain as much of NCLB's federal control over testing and accountability as possible—and questioning the motives of those who wanted Washington to back off.

Discovering the joys of power is not a partisan phenomenon. The Republican George W. Bush administration suffered from the same problem. In 2002 or 2003, not long after the enactment of No Child Left Behind, I was out West with a high-ranking Bush education official. He was a former state superintendent and we were musing on what the law meant for state leaders (at the time, legislators in Utah and Connecticut were seeking to opt out of the law).

He said, "Rick, I'll tell you what. Some stuff in there will drive any state chief crazy. NCLB was a big, messy compromise. There are parts that would have had me kicking and screaming in my old job. But my job now is to make the law work. States are like frogs in a wheelbarrow: if we let that first one hop out, others will follow. So my job is not to let any of them jump."

That's the thing about power. When you have it, it's tempting to use it. Heck, you feel *obliged* to use it, even if you used to feel differently. When reformers come into authority, they suddenly find great wisdom in the words of Frank Underwood, the power-hungry protagonist of the television show *House of Cards*: "There are two types of vice presidents: doormats and matadors. Which do you think I intend to be?"[1]

Once in power, everyone's impulse is to be the matador. Otherwise, they feel like they're wasting an opportunity.

I get it. When you're in a position of authority, people expect you to act accordingly. I'm as prone to this as anyone (which is one reason I shy away from positions of authority). Years ago, I spent a week traveling across South Korea for the US State Department, meeting with Ministry of Education staff and talking to educational leaders. I was having a swell time opining on all manner of educational questions. But I did one public briefing that still makes me shake my head. Asked about South Korea's higher education reforms, I somehow wound up on a tangent about the benefits of the geographic dispersion of US universities and the possible lessons for Seoul-centric South Korea.

While I didn't actually know what I was talking about, it all sounded vaguely plausible. The next morning, my interpreter greeted me with a newspaper opened to my headshot and a lot of text. The story was in Korean, but it apparently reported on the American expert urging the government to revamp its approach to higher education reform. The ministry called and we headed back over to confer. The funniest thing? I resented the criticism and pushback we encountered at the ministry. Bizarrely, I realized I was now emotionally invested in this spur-of-the-moment, tossed-off notion. In twenty-four hours, it had become my baby. I'd like to say that this was a freak occurrence. I'm afraid I can't. Authority and influence can be heady things.

This doesn't just apply to national capitals, of course. In school systems, new superintendents routinely arrive with packed agendas. Communities want to know that they've hired a matador who'll make a difference. Leaders show they're up to the task by promising a slate of new reforms.

As I've mentioned, in my book *Spinning Wheels* I reported that urban school districts launched an average of eleven major reforms in a single three-year period—one every three months. The result: new reforms get plopped atop old, yielding layer upon layer of sediment, with teachers squashed beneath it all.[2]

Fresh-faced newbies may throw themselves into the latest reform. But they soon learn to close their door and trust that this one will fade out like so many others. In this way, the temptations of bureaucracy have helped to render schools reform-resistant—like a strain of virulent superflu.

This "superflu problem" highlights the value of measures that allow reform to unfurl in pristine settings. New schools or teacher preparation programs are free to adopt new curricula, instructional models, or staffing arrangements without having to cram them into reform-weary systems. The ability to start fresh permits a rare degree of coherence and focus.

Big-*R* Reformers and little-*r* reformers alike have celebrated this dynamic. Over the past decade, though, a funny thing happened: The more big-*R* Reformers found themselves in positions of authority, the more they felt called upon to specify what constitutes an acceptable teacher evaluation system or alternative licensure program. The result was a lot of new requirements and directives.

The same reformers who once sought to combat stifling bureaucracy have slowly become a new breed of bureaucrats. Of course, as you'd expect, they don't see it that way. That's not because they're innately bossy; it's more a function of where they now sit.

When working in schools, it's easy to remember that execution is what matters most. You're reminded daily that, done poorly, a promising curriculum or disciplinary policy is no help at all. You instinctively focus on the minute things that happen in classrooms and hallways. The risk, of course, is losing perspective and getting unduly excited about trivial tinkering. When you're in a foundation, in a state capital, or in Washington, the opposite can happen. Small successes can start to seem insignificant. Only sweeping policy change, with all of the attendant mandates and directives, seems worthwhile. This is how a movement of unshacklers and builders can quite accidentally become a movement of bureaucrats. This would be less of an issue if those in power recognized the problem. Unfortunately, as Allan Cohen and David Bradford, coauthors of *Influence Without Authority*, have observed, power tends to make us deaf (and fear of offending the powerful makes everyone else mute).[3] When you're in charge, you're confident that you're doing the right thing. You're surrounded by hangers-on, sycophants, and subordinates offering affirmation. It's easy to regard criticism as evidence that the critic has an agenda or just doesn't get it.

The costs of bureaucracy are easy to overlook or take for granted. But they're real, even when they go unnoticed. Here's a simple example. The

KIPP charter schools are generally deemed one of the more compelling reform successes of the past quarter-century. KIPP has played a profound role in making the case that low-income students can thrive academically and in demonstrating the potential of charter schooling. Yet a suffocating swath of rules almost kept KIPP from ever getting off the ground.

KIPP started as a single fifth-grade class within a Houston district school. When KIPP first sought to add students, just finding space was a challenge. Cofounder Mike Feinberg recounts:

> [S]upporters tried to get us buildings, and were told no. No buildings. No modulars. No classrooms beyond what we already had. We had one option left: for me to take our case all the way up to the Houston district superintendent at the time, Rod Paige, who went on to become the U.S. Secretary of Education. I tried and failed to get an appointment with him, so I decided to stalk him . . . One hot afternoon, I sat on the bumper of his car in the district parking lot and waited for four hours until he showed up. He seemed surprised and impressed by my crazy stunt, and set me up to meet with district representatives who were able to get us the space we needed.[4]

When you're sitting on the hot bumper, you can't help but see the costs of bureaucracy. When you're inside the air-conditioned offices, it's all too easy to lose sight of them. That's when it's crucial to know whether your vision of reform is about emancipating education or simply replacing yesterday's bureaucratic directives with your own.

10

What Research Can Really Tell Us

WE WERE IN MY GEORGETOWN graduate seminar on education policy. One student was making an impassioned case that lawmakers don't pay nearly enough attention to research.

She said, "We need to do what's been proven to work. Policy should be informed by research. The children deserve it."

People were nodding. I said, "Sounds reasonable. Of course, that also means we need to be sure about what works. Say a bit about that. What's an example of a policy that works?"

"We just need to pay attention to the research," she said. "For example, teacher evaluation works. Using observations and student performance to evaluate teachers and help them improve. That works."

I looked around the room and asked, "Anybody have a reaction?"

Another student, a former teacher, raised her hand. "We had a terrible evaluation system where I taught," she said. "I don't think it worked. I think it was a waste of time."

"I mean *good* teacher evaluation," the first student clarified. "Obviously, it has to be done well. But when it is, it works."

Shortly after, I paused the discussion to point out two things. The first was that, at least to my mind, there's not much in the way of research "proving" that teacher evaluation works. I believe that it's useful to evaluate employees and that this can help them to improve, but it's hard to find evidence to "prove" that.

The second is that saying "good" teacher evaluation helps is like saying "good" medicine helps. It's true, but it doesn't tell us anything. "Good" is just a label we affix to stuff that's helpful or that we like. The real question is whether research can teach us how to make stuff that is consistently "good." That turns out to be trickier than we might wish.

I'm going to offer a few thoughts on what research can teach us. I'll start, though, by encouraging you to be a bit nervous whenever a school reformer promises to do "what the research shows." After all, twentieth-century researchers reported that head size was a good measure of intelligence, girls were incapable of doing advanced math, and retardation was rampant among certain ethnic groups. You're probably thinking: "That wasn't real research!" Well, it was conducted by university professors, published in scholarly papers, and discussed in textbooks. Other than the fact that the findings now seem wacky, that sure sounds like "real research" to me.

Medical researchers, for instance, change their minds on important findings with distressing regularity. Even with their deep pockets and fancy lab equipment, they've gone back and forth on things like the dangers of cholesterol, the virtues of flossing, whether babies should sleep on their backs, how much exercise we should get, and the effects of alcohol. Things would be messy if lawmakers or insurers were expected to change policies in response to every new medical study.

In truth, science is frequently a lot less absolute than we imagine. In 2015, an attempt to replicate ninety-seven psychology studies with statistically significant results found that more than a third couldn't be duplicated.[1] More than 90 percent of psychology researchers admit to at least one behavior that might compromise their research, such as stopping data collection early because they liked the results, or not disclosing all of a study's conditions. And more than 40 percent admit having sometimes decided whether to exclude data based on what it would do to the results.[2]

Rigorous research will eventually influence policy and practice, but it's typically after a long and gradual accumulation of evidence. Perhaps the most famous example is with the health effects of tobacco, where a cumulative body of research ultimately swayed the public and shaped policy on smoking—in spite of tobacco companies' frenzied, richly funded efforts to suppress it. The consensus that emerged involved dozens of studies by hundreds of researchers, with consistent findings piling up over decades.

When school reformers assert that something "works," that's hardly ever what they have in mind. Rather, such claims are usually based on a handful of recent studies—or even a single analysis—conducted by a small coterie of researchers. (In education, those researchers are not infrequently also advocates for the programs or policies they're evaluating.) When someone claims they can prove that extended learning time, school turnarounds, pre-K, or teacher residencies "work," what they usually mean is that they can point to a couple of studies that show some benefits from carefully executed pilot programs.

The upshot: when pilots suggest that policies or programs "work," it can mean a lot less than reformers might like.

Why might that be?

Think about it this way. The "gold standard" for research in medicine and social science is a randomized control trial (RCT). In an RCT, half of participants are randomly selected to receive the treatment—let's say a drug for high blood pressure. Both the treatment and control groups follow the same diet and health care plan. The one wrinkle is that the treatment group also receives the new drug. Because the drug is the only difference in care between the two groups, it can be safely credited with any significant difference in outcomes.

RCTs specify the precise treatment, who gets it, and how it is administered. This makes it relatively easy to replicate results. If patients in a successful RCT got a 100 milligram dosage of the blood pressure drug every twelve hours, that's how doctors should administer it in order to obtain the same results. If doctors gave out twice the recommended dosage, or if patients got it half as often as recommended, you wouldn't expect the same results. When we say that the drug "works," we mean that it has specific, predictable effects when used precisely.

At times, that kind of research can translate pretty cleanly to education. If precise, step-by-step interventions are found to build phonemic awareness or accelerate second-language mastery, replication can be straightforward.

For such interventions, research really can demonstrate "what works." And we should pay close attention.

This also helps illuminate the limits of research when it comes to reform, given all of the complexities and moving parts involved in system change. New policies governing things like class size, pre-K, or teacher pay get adopted and implemented by states and systems in lots of different ways. New initiatives are rarely precise imitations of promising pilots, even on those occasions when it's clear precisely what the initial intervention, dosage, design, and conditions were.

If imitators are imprecise and inconsistent, there's no reason to expect that results will be consistent. Consider class size reduction. For decades, advocates of smaller class sizes have pointed to findings from the Student Teacher Achievement Ratio (STAR) project, an experiment conducted in Tennessee in the late 1980s. Researchers found significant achievement gains for students in very small kindergarten and first grade classes. Swayed by the results, California legislators adopted a massive class-size reduction program that cost billions in its first decade. But the evaluation ultimately found no impact on student achievement.[3]

What happened? Well, what "worked" on a limited scale in Tennessee played out very differently when adopted statewide in California. The "replication" didn't actually replicate much beyond the notion of "smaller classes." Where STAR's small classes had thirteen to seventeen students, California's small classes were substantially larger. STAR was a pilot program in a few hundred classrooms, minimizing the need for new teachers, while California's statewide adoption required a tidal wave of new hires. Districts were forced to hire thousands of teachers who previously wouldn't have made the cut, while schools cannibalized art rooms and libraries in order to find enough classrooms to house them. Children who would have had better teachers in slightly larger classrooms were now in slightly smaller classrooms with worse teachers. It's no great shock that the results disappointed.

When reforms "work" in one setting, it's typically because of how all the pieces work in concert. Simply plopping "smaller classes" down in a new setting doesn't guarantee anything.

This can be hard for researchers to acknowledge because it strikes at the heart of their expertise. A few years ago, Nobel Prize–winning economist James Heckman savaged columnist George Will for questioning the benefits of expanded pre-K education. Early childhood education clearly works, Heckman insisted, based on his "evidence-based analysis of more than 30 years of data" from the Perry Preschool program. "It is as good a trial for effectiveness as those we currently rely on to evaluate prescription and over-the-counter drugs," he wrote.[4]

I hate to quarrel with a guy who won a Nobel Prize, but Heckman got this one wrong. The trial for preschool effectiveness tells us much less than do those drug trials. The ingredients of an over-the-counter drug can be replicated exactly and administered to new patients with precise directions. Preschool programs? Not so much. In fact, it's not all that clear just what the intervention is. Is it attending any preschool? Probably not. Is it attending any "high-quality" preschool? If so, precisely what made the Perry Preschool "high-quality"? Was it student-teacher ratio? Home visits? Teacher quality? All of these? None of these? Parsing those details is a pain, but it's exactly what's needed if one is going to claim that early childhood education—and not just the Perry program—"works."

We should be equally hesitant to decide that something *doesn't* work based on a single study. A pioneering 2010 merit pay study comes to mind. Conducted by talented researchers at Vanderbilt University, the study examined a three-year experiment in Nashville in which middle school math teachers were offered bonuses of up to $15,000 per year based on student test score gains. When the researchers found that the bonuses didn't significantly affect test scores, the results were widely interpreted to show that merit pay "doesn't work."[5]

You know what? The findings didn't affect my views one bit. I continue to think paying more money to terrific teachers is a good idea and that judging teachers based on test scores is a bad one. The study asked whether a cash bonus led to higher test scores. But merit pay can work in at least three ways: by encouraging teachers to work harder to boost tested performance, helping systems retain good teachers, or attracting talented people to the profession. The study assessed one crude approach to one piece of this, but was treated as providing a far more conclusive verdict.

Don't get me wrong. The study was fine. It taught us some useful things—including that paying teachers like insurance salesmen didn't raise test scores, at least in Nashville circa 2010. What doesn't exist anywhere, in any field, though, is research that tells us the "right" way to pay people. And don't expect it any time soon, because compensation systems are always shaped by culture, context, and human judgment. That makes things incredibly challenging for researchers. The trick is valuing research for what it can teach, without expecting it to necessarily determine what "works."

Undue deference to research can short-circuit plain old common sense. This is the problem with saying, "The research says . . . " People frequently tell me that "the research says" things that it doesn't, in fact, say. Much of the time, saying "the research says x" is just shorthand for "I think x makes sense." That would be fine, except that claiming the research says it masks our uncertainty, shuts down fruitful discussion, and blinds us to real-world complexity. It declares that anyone who disagrees is anti-science. That's not good.

We know less than we'd like about "what works" when it comes to education policy. In saying that, I'm *not* suggesting that we don't know anything. We know quite a bit. Research has taught us a lot, from how long teachers stay in a job to the average effect of snow days on student achievement. And keep in mind that research is only one way that we learn about the world. We also learn through personal experiences, observing others, received wisdom, and much else. All of these have value.

In fact, if life experience has led you to believe that smaller classes or merit pay are good ideas, I'd be surprised if a solitary study of a single locale were to cause you to reverse your views. Suggesting that policy or practice should be "based on research" presumes that the research is compelling enough and definitive enough to override a lifetime of accumulated knowledge. That *should* represent a pretty high bar. And be honest with yourself. If you expect someone else to change a deeply held belief because of a research finding, be sure that you would be equally willing to do so based on similar evidence.

I want to be clear: established bodies of rigorous evidence should be treated accordingly. Descriptive research is invaluable for providing hard data to inform discussion of teacher evaluation, bullying, or charter school performance. But well-meaning reformers frequently overstate what we know about "what works." Used carelessly, research can impair good judgment, lead reformers to imagine that "research-based" reforms guarantee much more than they do, and cause reformers to focus on *whether* reforms are adopted while shortchanging *how* they are adopted. And that's not good for anyone.

11

The Common Core's Uncommon Travails

AFTER YEARS OF BITTER BATTLES over the Common Core, it's hard to remember that advocates initially thought the whole thing was a no-brainer. Once upon a time, it was laughable to suggest that the Common Core might wind up being controversial. I know this because I used to get laughed at when I'd suggest it.

The Common Core started out modestly enough. When launched in 2009 and 2010, it was a document full of nice words about what students needed to learn in math and English language arts. Hardly anyone had heard of it, and those few who had were all pretty much on board. It was sponsored by the National Governors Association and the Council of Chief State School Officers. It had eager philanthropic support; backing from President Obama, the teachers unions, and the US Chamber of Commerce; and no obvious enemies. What could go wrong?

To answer that question, it helps to rewind the clock to 2001. The brand-new No Child Left Behind Act required that states adopt reading and math standards and test all students on these standards once a year in grades 3 to 8 (and once in high school). The law, however, left it to states to decide what standards and tests to use.

The result: states adopted very different standards, tests, and expectations. State leaders quickly realized they could post seemingly impressive results by adopting easy tests and setting a low bar for passage. States that adopted tough tests or set a high bar wound up making their schools look bad. This created a big incentive to dumb down the tests.

Obviously, this wasn't what anyone had intended. In response, some advocates, state leaders, and philanthropists started to talk about creating common reading and math tests that states could use. That would require common standards. And those discussions gave rise to the Common Core.

Common standards would allow interested states to develop a common test and to set common expectations for student performance, eliminating the opportunity for states to game the system. They would make it simple to compare the performance of schools, students, and educators, as well as the effects of different instructional resources and strategies. And they would make things easier for families that moved across state lines by ensuring more consistent instruction.

Even better, the whole thing would be voluntary, avoiding the old 1990s-era fights over national standards. States would be free to participate or not. And it was promised that the Common Core wouldn't determine curriculum or *how* teachers taught—states, school districts, schools, and educators would still be free to make those decisions. Common Core advocates imagined that maybe one or two dozen states would run with all this, and that the others would go about their business as usual.

I still remember the day that David Coleman, who shepherded the Common Core into existence, walked me through the draft standards. Coleman is a friend, an idea-a-minute dynamo, and a ridiculously smart guy. We must have spent two hours talking our way through the new standards. The conversation brought to mind a time when I was wandering through a Midwestern city in the wee hours and came across a guy in a lawn chair, drinking a twelve-pack and gazing at a brand-new office building. Turned out he was the foreman, his crew had just finished construction, and he was taking a night to admire their handiwork. He beamed the whole time in wonder at what he'd wrought. That's how Coleman looked that day as he flipped through the draft standards, pointing to features he especially liked. I left impressed by Coleman's passion and thinking that the standards themselves seemed perfectly reasonable.

Yet, within a few years, this innocuous, reasonable, and likable enterprise would sour. Critics would denounce the Common Core as "Obama-

Core," linking it to President Obama's controversial federal health care law. YouTube videos attacking Common Core homework would go viral. The fracas was especially striking because it was over frameworks for reading and math instruction—small beans compared to political clashes over health care, taxes, or terrorism. Why did things turn out this way?

While I won't drag you through the Common Core debate, I'll note that there were real issues to discuss (contrary to what supporters frequently insisted). For instance, the Common Core called for a series of major "instructional shifts." The shifts stipulated that "informational texts" (not fiction or poetry) should account for 50 percent of reading in elementary school and 70 percent of reading by the end of high school. "Close reading" of the kind favored by postmodern literary critics was to be the default model for reading instruction. "Conceptual math" (with the picture-heavy instruction that became fodder for those YouTube videos) was to be the foundation of math instruction. Advocates cheered these changes; critics blasted them. The point is that reasonable people could disagree about them.

The Common Core's problems started with what seemed, at the time, like a huge victory. In 2009, the Obama administration decided to make the Common Core a key element in its $4.35 billion Race to the Top program. States that promised to sign onto the Common Core had a giant leg up in this celebrated competition. This didn't mean that the Common Core was suddenly a federal program, but it did put Washington's fingerprints all over it. The US Department of Education also proceeded to spend $350 million in Race to the Top funds to create new Common Core–aligned tests, and then pushed states to adopt the Common Core if they wanted relief from NCLB's accountability mandates (especially the ludicrous stipulation that 100 percent of students be proficient in reading and math by 2014). In major speeches, such as the State of the Union Address, President Obama took credit for the widespread adoption of the standards. This all made the Common Core feel a lot like a federal initiative and inclined Obama's critics to view it as just another part of the president's agenda.

It wasn't just Obama's team making the whole endeavor seem less than wholly voluntary. There was the Gates Foundation's famed wall map tracking Common Core adoption. As state after state jumped on board in 2009 thanks to Race to the Top, the Gates offices were reportedly a whirlwind of whoops and high-fives. The Foundation spent tens of millions on Common Core advocacy and implementation.

These insistent efforts yielded a kind of "stealth" reform, in which states signed on without much grassroots understanding, enthusiasm, or support. There was no public consideration, legislative debate, or media scrutiny. Mostly, state boards of education quietly voted to adopt the standards. The Common Core was a fait accompli before most people had ever heard of it.

Advocates thought this meant things were going swimmingly. They kept telling me that these quiet victories were terrific; they were only too happy to sidestep messy, "political" distractions. I thought they were mistaken. As I wrote back then, "I'd be astonished if one American in fifty can tell you what the Common Core actually is and what it involves—hell, I'd be surprised if one in five educators or state legislators can do that. There are long rows of argument and persuasion still to be hoed. And, if you're eager to overhaul what gets taught in forty-odd states serving forty million or more students, that's probably as it should be."[1]

How one responds to pushback says a great deal about how one thinks about reform. The biggest mistake the Common Core advocates made, I think, was refusing to acknowledge or engage their critics. Remember, for better or worse, public education is (duh) a profoundly public enterprise. It involves other people's kids, money, and communities. If you hurriedly cram changes into place, it's a lot like submerging a beach ball in a pool. You can do it, but the harder you shove it under, the more forcefully it's going to pop back up.

Unfortunately for their cause, Common Core advocates didn't really expect anyone to push back. As Bill Gates told the *Washington Post* in 2014, after things had blown up, "These are not political things. These are where people are trying to apply expertise" to make education better.[2] If you think of trying to change what millions of kids are taught as just a matter of "applying expertise," you're not going to anticipate or understand pushback—which means that beach ball will be coming back in a hurry.

When critics argued that the Common Core was federally imposed, supporters could have acknowledged that Washington had elbowed its way into steering a state-led initiative, conceded the problem, and discussed ways to address it. When critics complained about the adoption process or the instructional shifts, their concerns could have been taken as a warning and a chance to address potential problems. Instead, advocates were eager to declare the debate over and move on to reshaping tests, curricula, homework, and teacher preparation.

When advocates did acknowledge the critics, they tended to dismiss them as ignorant kooks and misinformed cranks. Then-US Secretary of Education Arne Duncan famously told the nation's newspaper editors that critics were an irrational "fringe" and the nation's state superintendents that critics were "suburban white moms" fearful they'd learn that their precious babies weren't as special as they'd thought.[3] Similar dismissals were plentiful.

I saw an early but telling example of how reformers got this wrong in 2011, barely a year after the standards were officially released. In my role as executive editor of *Education Next*, I was putting together a forum assessing the Common Core math standards. We solicited serious people on both sides. Even at that early stage, the skeptics included the dean of an Ivy League ed school and the Texas commissioner of education. We ultimately invited a former official from the George W. Bush administration, who promptly agreed to critique the standards.

To make the case for the Common Core, I reached out to the guy who had worked with Coleman to oversee the creation of the math standards. After weeks of unanswered e-mails and unreturned calls, he finally told me he was too busy to write fifteen hundred words defending the standards. He suggested that I ask a colleague of his. After more delays and nonresponse, the colleague eventually demurred too. On it went until six proponents of Common Core math had declined to get paid to write four pages promoting their handiwork for one of the nation's most influential education publications. I've run the *Education Next* forums since 2001, and that was the only time that I've ever encountered such recalcitrance. The situation was bizarre, but revealing.

When you're pushing big changes to public systems, the burden is *supposed* to be on the would-be reformers. Even after winning a unanimous Supreme Court decision in *Brown v. Board of Education of Topeka* in 1954, civil rights advocates spent decades making and remaking their case. Charter school advocates have continuously argued their case since the first charter law was passed in 1991. Good, bad, or otherwise, that's how a free nation works.

Meanwhile, as the Common Core's polling numbers steadily eroded, foundations spent millions on "push-polls" that would inevitably report that 80 percent or more of the nation supported the Common Core. The pollsters managed this by asking questions like, "Do you support states voluntarily adopting high-quality, rigorous reading and math standards?" (I always wondered about the respondents who said "no.") Advocates would point to the numbers and say, "See, people really love the Common Core; they've just been duped by misinformation."

Of course, the problem with the push-polling was that the doubters didn't necessarily agree that the standards were high-quality or voluntary. It was like the potato-chip industry running a poll that asked, "Do you think healthy, nutritious potato chips should be part of any child's diet?" When you ask the question this way, you stack the deck—respondents think, "Hmm, if there are healthy, nutritious potato chips out there, then sure." But the question falls apart if people doubt that potato chips are healthy or nutritious.

Over time, Common Core advocates started playing a kind of political hardball that made things look distinctly less voluntary. In 2014, for instance, ExxonMobil's political action committee announced that it would no longer donate to public officials who opposed the Common Core. This did nothing to assuage critics who saw the Common Core as the handiwork of big government, big business, and big philanthropy.

The missteps took on a special poignancy because, by themselves, standards are kind of like the mission statement on the wall of a McDonald's or a Burger King. You know, where they promise fast and friendly service, quality ingredients, a welcoming environment, yada yada. Whether restaurants actually deliver on all this, of course, usually has little or nothing to do with those words hanging on the wall. What matters is what people are actually doing. It's the same thing with standards.

Even Common Core advocates conceded that standards are often a symbolic exercise, and that the new ones would matter only if they led to changes in testing, curriculum, and instruction. Bitter fights to adopt standards are self-defeating if victories come at the expense of the broad-based support needed to make those other changes happen. This is where the Common Core's early wins proved to be pyrrhic victories. By 2016, just twenty of the forty-five Common Core states were using a Common Core–aligned test. That number had fallen precipitously since 2012. The whole exercise had become a poisoned brand and fodder for late-night comics.

Though it would have been slower and less sweeping than advocates might have wished, the Common Core could have been piloted by the dozen or more states eager to leap on board in early 2009. Those states could have adopted the Common Core on their own timeline, designed a common test, and shown that it could work as envisioned. If things went smoothly, more states would have wanted in. This is how you set in motion a virtuous cycle, rather than the destructive one that has dominated a decade of education debate.

Astute reformers know that complaints always start at the fringe, whether the issue is foreign policy, police tactics, or schooling. Like sparks from a fire, these complaints by themselves don't much matter. What *does* matter is whether those sparks jump the clearing around the campfire and start to ignite the forest. We can ignore them or we can tend to the firebreak. It's our choice. In reform, tending the break requires anticipating problems, acknowledging concerns, and offering practical solutions. It's tempting to dismiss those initial sparks, but it's wiser to treat them as cautionary flares.

12

The False Promise of Court-Driven Reform

I WAS TALKING WITH a Republican governor who'd lit off some school reform fireworks in his state. We were at a conference in Atlanta, and his staff had arranged for us to meet in a convenient hotel. The conference room smelled of stale doughnuts and wood polish.

He'd been pushing to revamp teacher tenure. He said, "I knew this would be hard, but it's still a lot harder than I expected. Even Republican legislators don't want to get crosswise with the teachers."

I nodded.

He said, "I'm wondering if it's even worth trying to legislate on this. It's using a lot of political capital and I'm not sure we'll get anywhere."

"What are you thinking?" I asked.

"Well," he said, "I've got these folks telling me that they can drive this through the courts with a carefully crafted lawsuit. They're saying that's a better way to go. I'm not usually one for going to the courts, but it seems like they can move the needle. You have any thoughts?"

As a matter of fact, I had a lot of thoughts on it. It's a question that looms large in school reform. Should reformers embrace the courts as an ally? How much faith should reformers put in judges to drive change?

After all, politics is messy, slow, and dumb. Reformers see that firsthand every day. Meanwhile, most of us have more experience with *Law & Order* reruns than real-life courtrooms. Especially for school reformers versed in the iconic legacy of *Brown v. Board of Education of Topeka*, courts summon images of crusading prosecutors and stouthearted defense attorneys. Judges can seem pleasingly smart, fair-minded, and able to get things done.

The courts promise swift justice, and not just on *Law & Order*. In the film *Legally Blonde*, crusading law student (and fashionista) Elle Woods clears the defendant of murder in a trial that takes no more than ten or fifteen minutes of screen time. Using her keen knowledge of hair care, Woods debunks the perm-related alibi of the accused's stepdaughter and ensures that justice is done. It beats the heck out of legislative stalemate.

So perhaps it's no great surprise that some big-R Reformers have turned to lawsuits to rewrite state policies. The most visible of these to date has been *Vergara v. California*, in which nine Los Angeles students charged in 2012 that the state's teacher tenure, due process, and seniority policies violated the state constitution.

Judge Rolf Treu ruled for the plaintiffs, finding that the policies stuck poor and minority students with lousy teachers who are almost impossible to fire. (Treu's verdict was eventually overturned by the California Court of Appeal, which ruled that the plaintiffs didn't show that the policies caused them particular harm.[1])

On one hand, Treu's decision was easy to like. In California, tenure, due process, and last-in, first-out policies have made it expensive and difficult to terminate even the one to three percent of California teachers deemed "grossly ineffective." Treu noted that dismissal of a single teacher can take up to a decade and cost upward of $450,000. He wrote in his decision that the evidence presented in his courtroom "shocks the conscience."[2]

At the time, big-R Reformers greeted the *Vergara* verdict with a *lot* of enthusiasm. As one influential California Democrat told me, "It's all about evidence. The rules of the courtroom force it. That's the great thing about the courts. It's all about the research and the truth. It's amazing to see. The politics and the arm-twisting are out."

Me? I saw things differently. I don't think judges are equipped to answer complex policy questions, referee competing evidentiary claims, or reform public agencies.

University of Colorado professor Josh Dunn puts it well: "For those wishing to use the courts to reform education, I bring bad news: courts are not good at it. Attempts to use courts to reform public institutions have largely failed, and education is the principle example . . . The history of education litigation could be summarized as one of good intentions leading to bad results."[3]

My lack of enthusiasm for *Vergara* struck many reformers as misguided. They explained that legislative efforts to revamp tenure in California were a dead end and something had to be done. As one advocate put it, "Rick, marriage equality was getting nowhere, so advocates took to the courts. The Supreme Court's decision in *Obergefell* changed the national landscape. Public opinion on gay marriage followed. That's how we ought to tackle school reform."

I get it, but I'm not sold. I see three big problems with the analogy.

First, the fight for gay marriage was about *access* to marriage, not the *quality* of a marriage. Courts are good at ensuring access. They can order a justice of the peace to file the paperwork and allow same-sex couples to marry. If a justice of the peace doesn't comply, she's breaking the law. It's pretty straightforward. On the other hand, if courts were asked to ensure that same-sex couples have a satisfactory wedding experience—or a happy marriage—that would be a whole different ballgame. Lawsuits like *Vergara* aren't about access to schooling. Instead, they are efforts to force alterations to state personnel policies in hopes of improving the *quality* of teaching.

Second, the act of legalizing gay marriage is relatively straightforward. Same-sex marriage is now constitutional. There. Done. That's not the case when the court orders that policies be altered. When that happens, the legislature may or may not comply. It may be unable or unwilling to enact the changes, and judges don't possess the authority to "make" legislatures adopt new policies. If the legislature does comply, the judge has to determine whether the changes are satisfactory. If not, he'll tell the legislature to try again. And around we go. Meanwhile, school systems need to figure out what to do about policies, practices, and contracts. Given the uncertainty and foot-dragging, decisions like *Vergara* are more likely to yield bureaucratic paralysis than dramatic action. Just look at New Jersey, which is in its *fifth decade* of back-and-forth in equity finance litigation.

The legal headaches and squabbling have fostered confusion, compliance, and timid leadership. That's not a recipe for terrific schools.

But that's how the gears of justice grind. Charles Dickens summed it up rather neatly in *Bleak House*, drolly describing a fictional case that had dragged out for generations: "Jarndyce and Jarndyce drones on. This scarecrow of a suit has, over the course of time, become so complicated, that no man alive knows what it means. . . . The little plaintiff or defendant, who was promised a new rocking-horse when Jarndyce and Jarndyce should be settled, has grown up, possessed himself of a real horse, and trotted away into the other world."[4] Most lawyers will confess that Dickens' wry take reflects their experiences more than *Legally Blonde* does.

Third, *Vergara* was a double-edged sword in a way that same-sex marriage wasn't. Champions of same-sex marriage had little fear that opponents could use their logic to strip same-sex couples of other rights. With *Vergara*, however, once judges start dictating what constitutes acceptable educational practice, there's no reason to stop at tenure laws. And there's no reason to assume that you'll like the substance of future verdicts. Indeed, within days of Treu's verdict, Kevin Welner, a professor at the University of Colorado and a vocal critic of the big-R Reform agenda, lamented the decision but enthused that courts could now use the precedent to micromanage transportation and buildings, restrict school choice, dictate accountability practices, and much more.[5] If the courts did so, many who cheered *Vergara* could feel very differently in a hurry.

The appropriate place to address these issues is in legislatures and school districts. Legislatures are where elected representatives write the laws by which citizens agree to abide. Legislators can negotiate and compromise; incorporate evidence, ideology, and experience as they see fit; and rewrite laws at a later date. They represent a range of views and concerns, and they can be voted out of office if their constituents disapprove of what they've done.

Courts lack all of these qualities. Courts are places where laws are applied to specific cases. They are poor venues for finding compromise. Judges are typically appointed with little in the way of democratic accountability. They're usually trained as lawyers and their expertise is in case law and legal processes. Judges cannot readily revisit or modify former decisions.

School reformers are dealing with complex issues rife with unintended consequences—exactly the kind of thing that courts are ill-equipped to handle.

While we might wish it were otherwise, the complexities of school improvement are better suited to legislative wrangling than to judicial declarations. For instance, while I believe that tenure and seniority policies are anachronistic and need to be rewritten, I think the issue is far less straightforward than Judge Treu imagined. Tenure does indeed stop schools from terminating some lousy teachers. At the same time, *good* teachers held accountable for student outcomes might be leery of going into high-poverty schools without the protections of tenure. The issue is less cut-and-dried than it might seem at first blush, and the courts are not a good place for hashing this out.

I can hear you asking, "But what about *Brown v. Board of Education* in 1954? Hasn't *that* had a profoundly positive impact?"

Sure. *Brown* was a landmark blow for educational equality. But, like *Obergefell*, *Brown* was about access. The Supreme Court said in *Brown* that the regime of "separate but equal" ratified by *Plessy v. Ferguson* six decades earlier was inherently unequal and that states could not deny black children access to "white" public schools.

Even on that reasonably uncomplicated question, though, keep in mind that, for more than a decade, *Brown* barely moved the needle on school integration. The verdict *was* symbolically powerful—hugely so when President Eisenhower sent National Guard troops to escort nine black students into Little Rock Central High School—but, for many years, its practical impact was remarkably modest. It took a series of cases over two decades, including *Brown II, Swann v. Charlotte-Mecklenburg Board of Education, Griffin v. County School Board of Prince Edward County, Coffey v. State Educational Finance Commission,* and *Brown v. South Carolina State Board of Education,* to even start accomplishing the relatively straightforward task *Brown* set out.

And let's not forget *Plessy* itself. In 1896, the US Supreme Court had ruled that "separate but equal" was perfectly constitutional. It's a reminder that courts can rule the "wrong" way, erecting barriers to reform that can stand for generations.

If it helps any, know that the messiness of politics is also a safeguard. It hampers our ability to make the changes we want, but it also reins in those people whom we deem misguided. The democratic process *is* painfully frustrating and slow, but it's also how we can marshal the public agreement that gives complex reforms a fighting chance to succeed.

By the way, even if the courts were a better venue for making social policy than they are, it turns out that they are also frustrating and slow. Four years after they first filed suit, *Vergara*'s plaintiffs had their final appeal rejected by the California Supreme Court in 2016. And that was relatively quick work: *Brown* only made it to the Supreme Court after decades of now-forgotten lawsuits. And don't overlook the case of Myra Clark Gaines, who filed a lawsuit in 1834 over an inheritance. After eight hearings by the Louisiana Supreme Court and sixteen by the US Supreme Court, the case wasn't settled until 1892—seven years after Gaines's death.

Sigh. Where is Elle Woods when you need her?

13

The Real Promise
of School Choice

FOR A LOT OF SCHOOL REFORMERS, how you feel about school choice is a quick gauge of whether you're a "reformer." If you like charter schools, you pass. If not . . . not so much.

I think of the foundation official who told me that he and his colleagues were looking to fund "reform-minded" researchers. He'd confessed that they didn't know much about education, so I asked how they knew whom to approach. "The first thing," he said, "is we look to see if they've studied charter schools."

There are lots of arguments for and against school choice. You've probably heard them all. Proponents argue that it can provide an opportunity for kids to escape lousy schools, a chance for families to find schools that reflect their values, and incentives for all schools to do better. Skeptics fear the impact on racial segregation, students left behind in troubled schools, and civic values.

I don't want to wade into these debates right now. What I do want to discuss is the real promise of school choice, at least as I see it—which is something that often gets lost in the reflexive back-and-forth. I want to talk about why school choice reflects a humane, organic vision of school improvement and what's required for it to deliver on that promise.

I know that talking about school choice as "humane" and "organic" can sound strange. After all, choice is routinely pilloried as part of a "neoliberal corporatist" conspiracy, and its defenders most often make their case in mechanistic terms: arguing that choice lifts reading and math scores, and therefore that it "works." (Critics respond that the results are mixed or modest, and therefore that choice "doesn't work.") But I think that such exchanges largely miss the mark. School choice is not an intervention. It's not a pill you take. Rather, it's a chance to reach into the medicine cabinet and grab a bottle. Whether that will help depends on what's in that cabinet.

The promise of choice is not that, tomorrow, schools will magically be "better." The promise of markets and choice-based systems—whether we're talking computers, cars, or schools—is that, over the long haul, they create room to innovate, problem-solve, and build. They can empower educators and families to create and choose better schools.

The logic becomes easier to grasp if you spend much time talking school improvement with principals or district leaders. Conversations are peppered with phrases like, "I'd like to do this, but the contract requires . . . " "I'd like to pay them more, but HR says . . . " and "I'd love to move those dollars, but we're not allowed . . . " Educators wrestle with inherited rules, regulations, and contract provisions that may no longer make sense but that can be extraordinarily difficult to change. Even when formally allowed to act, school and system leaders are hamstrung by ingrained customs and culture.

School choice can make it easier for educators to pioneer new school models, for successful models to grow, and for unsuccessful efforts to fade away. By allowing more families to access private options, school vouchers and education savings accounts make it possible for educators and entrepreneurs to open schools that cater to these families' preferences. Charter schooling enables educators to get a new school approved without having to spend years pleading with district officials for flexibility, facilities, and a go-ahead.

Old organizations frequently struggle to manage change. They grow rigid with time, which makes it difficult to take advantage of new technology or address changing needs. This is just as true of companies as it is of school systems. The private sector's secret in addressing this is not that old companies are especially nimble—it's that those that can't keep up give way to new entrants. The list of giant companies that have gone bankrupt over time is pretty staggering; in fact, the average life span for a Fortune 500 company is just fifty years.[1] Many school systems are two or three times that old. When we tell educators that their only way forward is to "fix" aged systems or schools, we put them in a nearly impossible position.

In most of life, we take for granted that once-dominant companies will lose their way. Think of Circuit City or Pan Am, Myspace or Blockbuster. It's not that once-successful executives get dumb. Rather, it's that these companies establish staffing models, support systems, contracts, and business practices that work great—until they no longer do. When this happens, it turns out to be remarkably tough to "reform" the old model. Markets allow for new problem solvers to emerge and meet new needs in new ways. If it's hard for taxi companies to adapt their model to the job-sharing economy, entrepreneurs can invent new models like Uber or Lyft.

Airbnb is a website that allows people to rent out rooms. It was started in 2007 by two Rhode Island School of Design alums who wanted to rent out their loft. Dissatisfied with the existing websites linking potential renters with available rooms, they designed their own. They posted pictures of their loft, featuring three air mattresses and the promise of a homemade breakfast. With a major design conference in town, they landed three renters at $80 a head. After that, they started getting emails asking when their site would list rooms around the world. Cofounder Joe Gebbia observed, "While solving our own problem, we were solving someone else's problem too . . . People told us what they wanted, so we set off to create it." By 2014, Airbnb was listing over 550,000 properties around the world.[2]

In education, room for new entrants can enable that same kind of reinvention. Charter schools like Arizona's Carpe Diem and California's Summit Public Schools offer a nice illustration.[3] Rick Ogston founded Carpe Diem after coming to education from stints as a Marine, a family therapist, and a church pastor. He brought a fresh perspective and designed the school largely through trial and error. Today, Carpe Diem features a blended learning model for grades 6–12, with student time split between individualized online instruction and teacher-led collaborative workshops. Making this work, says Ogston, meant changing "the entire ecosystem," including the roles of teachers, parents, students, and administrators. The design enables teachers to work with multiple grade levels and the same students for successive years. Because routine content delivery, practice, and assessment are done via computer, teachers have a lot of time for one-on-one or small group instruction. Plenty of district leaders talk about doing such things, but it's a whole lot easier to do it successfully if you're a startup working from a fresh sheet of paper. Carpe Diem's half-dozen schools post impressive academic results, attract enthusiastic families, and operate at a lower cost per pupil than nearby district schools.

Diane Tavenner, founder and CEO of Summit Public Schools, tells a similar story. She founded Summit, which also serves students in grades 6–12, for a simple reason: "The factory model [in public schools] wasn't working." At the outset, Summit "adopted every best practice or research finding that we could possibly apply . . . Yet there were pieces where we felt like we weren't getting where we wanted to be." Eight years in, Summit piloted a self-directed learning model and moved every assignment and handout online, making them accessible at any time to parents and teachers. Summit now runs nearly a dozen schools, with terrific results. None of this would have been possible without rethinking the role of teachers and leveraging new technology.

Now, you're probably sitting there thinking, "Swell, but any school district could do what Carpe Diem or Summit did." Well, it's also true that any big travel company could have done what Airbnb did. But they didn't. That's because it's hard for established organizations to fundamentally rethink their work, marshal the will to implement sweeping change, or convince employees to embrace it. An organization's culture and DNA reflect certain assumptions about pay levels, work hours, expectations, job descriptions, offices, hiring, and the rest. This makes it incredibly difficult to say, "Guess what, everyone? We're starting from scratch! We're totally changing what you do, how you're paid, who's in charge of your team, and how we configure our schools and classrooms." So while districts can theoretically do what Carpe Diem or Summit did, they generally don't. And if they do, they usually have trouble doing it well.

It's not like districts never change. They change all the time. But the changes tend to be cosmetic and inch-deep, precisely because bigger changes create a lot of discomfort and usually require modifying existing rules, contracts, and routines. This can make it prohibitive to launch a new school or reconfigure an old one. Before they can even get started, educators seeking transformative change have to exhaust themselves just battling for permission to act. The result: people tinker, convince themselves their tinkering is more significant than it is, and hope that'll do the trick.

School choice makes it far easier to start new schools, which can settle on a clear and coherent purpose from the outset. New schools can adopt the kinds of instructional programs, calendars, and staffing models they want without having to unwind what's already there or court skeptical stakeholders.

That kind of coherence is crucial. Terrific schools are typically defined by a shared set of expectations, a faculty that's committed to the school's mission, and students and families who broadly agree on what they want from the school. While this kind of agreement doesn't guarantee success, it's tough for schools to thrive without it.

But the success of school choice turns on having the ecosystem in place that can cultivate and support good new schools. Silicon Valley is a hotbed of innovation not because it has "markets" but because it has an ecosystem of researchers, investors, talent, social capital, and expertise that fuels promising ventures. Markets are organic, dynamic things, and a place like Silicon Valley offers a fertile environment.

Since their launch in the early 1990s, charter schooling and school voucher programs have enjoyed real success, though far less than they might have. I think this is partly because advocates spent so much energy insisting that choice "works" that they didn't bother doing much about the ecosystem that would help choice *to* work. I first noticed this back in 1999, when I spent a lot of time in Milwaukee for a book I was researching on school choice.

At the time, because of its pioneering voucher program, Milwaukee was the epicenter of the national school choice debate. When I first arrived in the city, I expected to see proponents feverishly nurturing an ecosystem where choice would flourish. I'd imagined advocates would be wooing promising new school founders, helping schools find facilities, securing financing, addressing legal and logistical issues, and recruiting teachers and leaders.

Instead, choice schools were mostly left to fend for themselves. Proponents had scraped together the resources to support, in a ramshackle old house, a couple of one-person operations that did their best to provide schools with legal advice, operational support, and political coordination. While the effort was admirable, the result was like asking two guys with a shovel and a wrench to build a new baseball stadium. The results were disappointingly (if predictably) mixed.

In the private sector, new ventures routinely tap into a web of providers that offer services, financing, and advice. That infrastructure didn't exist for schools in Milwaukee. Why? Well, there'd never been much call for it. For school choice to thrive, reformers had to erect the scaffolding that the private sector typically takes for granted.

Over time, choice supporters have gotten better at understanding and addressing all this. The best example may be New Orleans, where Hurricane Katrina shut down the school system for a full year in 2005. The vacuum that resulted was filled mostly with charter schools, whose impressive results have been well documented. Less well documented is the role reformers played in building the ecosystem that helped launch and support those schools. A pipeline of talented teachers and school leaders, generous philanthropic support, and the nonprofit New Schools for New Orleans played crucial roles in everything from recruiting new school leaders to locating facilities.

Choice skeptics will inevitably note that the same opportunities that allow the Ogstons and Tavenners to create great schools can enable con artists and incompetents. It's a fair point. Reform is always about balancing costs and benefits, which is why thoughtful people are going to disagree. I think the benefits of school choice are likely to outweigh these costs. Others will disagree.

By the way, the concern about shysters and bunglers helps explain the appeal of charter schooling, with its promise that authorizers will keep a firm hand on which schools get approved and will shutter those that deserve it. This makes a lot of sense. One hazard, of course, is that the promise to ratchet up oversight can lead authorizers to increasingly dictate school practices regarding things like discipline or special education. Unchecked, that impulse will eventually lead authorizers to recreate the bureaucracies that stymie educators in traditional systems. I don't have any especially good answers to this dilemma, other than vigilance and common sense.

Calls for oversight are motivated in large part by the fear that parents will choose poorly. After all, parents make lots of decisions that may strike an observer as dubious. Some are mostly a matter of judgment (like letting your six-year-old have dessert before dinner) while others are more self-evidently irresponsible (like letting your six-year-old play with a chainsaw). The reality is that some parents will inevitably choose schools for their children that we wouldn't choose for ours.

As researchers have documented, parents have a habit of showing less interest in test scores than some observers think they should.[4] The question is whether, in choosing schools with scores that reformers deem too low, parents are being irresponsible. Maybe. But maybe not. Perhaps it's simply a matter of judgment. Those scores may be incomplete or misleading, and it's hardly unreasonable for parents to favor schools based on the fact that their child is growing more disciplined, assertive, or interested in school. These are thorny questions. Reasonable people will disagree, and that's okay.

In the end, the right way to think about choice is not as Dr. Pendergrast's Miracle Salve but as an opportunity for educators, entrepreneurs, and parents to create better schools. That's why, if school choice is to deliver on its promise, reformers need to spend more time asking what it takes to help terrific schools flourish—and less insisting that school choice "works."

14

Getting Technology Right

YOU WANT TO SHOW you're a big-time reformer? Be sure to say "ed tech" rather than "education technology." Name-drop new virtual school models. Talk excitedly about learning management systems and coding boot camps. The sad thing is that I'm only half kidding.

Whenever I catch myself doing this, it reminds me that, for some reason, talk of technology causes reformers' brains to freeze up like an old Microsoft operating system.

With education technology, the details change but the wide-eyed enthusiasm stays the same. Whether the latest fad is Internet connectivity, laptop computers, smartboards, tablets, iPhones, televisions, or ballpoint pens, breathless reformers insist that the world is about to change. Eventually, though, we realize that all the new stuff hasn't made much difference. Teachers are teaching the same way, and students are learning the same amount. Things simmer down for a bit, then the whole cycle starts anew. This phenomenon has been recounted in a shelf full of depressing books, though my favorite may be Larry Cuban's *Oversold and Underused*.[1]

Schooling's dismal track record doesn't reflect how technology plays out in most of our lives. Technology usually makes our lives more convenient and comfortable. It opens the door to new experiences. There are the obvious examples like the microwave, x-ray, airplane, and computer. But there are also lots of less dramatic cases, like the bundle of tech tools used to create Uber, the ride-sharing service that reshaped urban transit. Dreamed up during a Paris conference when its cofounders were having trouble finding a cab, Uber launched in 2010 and employed more than a million drivers in fifty-eight countries by 2015.

Cofounder Travis Kalanick talks about Uber's convenience and cost, noting, "In most cities, UberX [the company's taxi equivalent] is half the cost of a taxi and when you factor in parking, insurance and maintenance, commuting with UberX is cheaper than owning a car."[2] What made this breakthrough possible? Well, it turns out that Uber's technology isn't complex; in fact, it was all widely available when Uber launched. Kalanick and cofounder Garrett Camp's contribution was figuring out how to combine geo-location, mapping software, push notifications, and mobile payments in order to help people get around more cheaply and easily.

The big taxi companies, with all their money and market share, had access to everything that Uber did. But they were doing just fine under the old order and so had limited incentive to change. And taxi commissions and existing regulations restricted their pricing, service provision, and use of drivers and cars, which limited their ability to change. Plus, since they already had their old cabs, drivers, dispatchers, cost structures, and routines, they found it easiest to "innovate" by stitching technology on top of what they already did—by giving dispatchers new computers or installing new video screens in cabs.

In terms of incentives, constraints, and innovation, schools have long approached technology a lot more like taxi companies than like Uber. As a result, ed tech tends to be more sizzle than substance.

Nearly a century ago, in 1922, Thomas Edison proclaimed, "The motion picture is destined to revolutionize our educational system . . . In a few years it will supplant largely, if not entirely, the use of textbooks."[3] Not so much. Soon enough, radio was the hot new thing. In 1931, US Commissioner of Education William Cooper established a radio section in the US Office of Education and, by 1932, nine states were broadcasting regular educational programs. Benjamin Darrow, author of *Radio: The Assistant Teacher*, touted radio as the "vibrant and challenging textbook of the air."[4] I could tell similar stories about TV, the desktop computer, laptops, tablets, and so on.

The problem is not with the technology (most of these same devices have worked pretty well outside of schools) but with how it's used. Technology is grafted onto schools and classrooms while the rules and routines governing classroom design, scheduling, staffing, and pedagogy remain unchanged. This is not a recipe for reinvention.

Several years ago, the School District of Philadelphia partnered with Microsoft to design and launch a $60 million "School of the Future." Even with Microsoft's expertise and the chance to design a twenty-first-century school from scratch, the results were underwhelming. My friend Mary Cullinane, who was running education for Microsoft at the time, told me about one of the project's first design meetings. Mary had assumed that everyone would start by talking about teaching and learning. "But you know what we started with?" she asked. "Ceiling-mounted projectors!" The technology became a distracting fascination rather than an opportunity to reimagine schooling. (Mary and I later teamed up to do a book on the School of the Future, which mostly illustrated how routine stuff like job posting rules can stymie an ambitious school redesign.)

It's distressingly common for technology to be more of a shiny distraction than a difference-maker. In fact, as learning scientist extraordinaire Bror Saxberg and I argued in *Breakthrough Leadership in the Digital Age*, we know of only one technology that has fundamentally transformed teaching and learning: the book.[5]

The book first became available to the masses in the mid-1400s with the invention of the printing press. Before that, teachers and students relied on painstakingly hand-inscribed parchment. As statistician Nate Silver has observed, "Almost overnight, the cost of producing a book decreased by about three hundred times, so a book that might have cost $20,000 in today's dollars instead cost $70."[6] The availability of books skyrocketed.

Educators didn't exactly welcome the printing press. Why? Well, schools were predominantly church-run affairs, and religious leaders fretted about the lack of guidance for readers left to their own devices. There were also fears that printed books would be a poor substitute for scribe-copied, meticulously ornamented books. Abbot Johannes Trithemius lamented the loss of "devotion to the writing of sacred texts."[7]

Over time, though, educators came to cherish the book. It gave students access to experts from around the world, so they no longer had to depend solely on their teachers for knowledge. Before the book, there was no good way to convey knowledge other than by teachers telling students things. This had restricted what teachers could do and the ways in which they might teach. The book made it possible for students to learn at home or on their own.

Books allowed students to move at their own pace. Students could re-read passages as needed, giving them more time to absorb confusing content or master tricky concepts. Books made it possible for students to learn at night, when ill, or even when studying with an inept teacher. Now, it's true that books might have been inferior to a lesson delivered by a phenomenal instructor or read in a scribed manuscript. Most of the time, though, and for most students, books were a vast improvement over the alternative.

When I teach college today, it's hard for me to imagine a world before the book. Much of what I do is ask students to read things so that we can discuss, debate, and make sense of them. If books weren't around, there'd be little time for any of that because I'd spend most of class just telling students stuff. When I taught high school, I found it tough enough to keep all the students engaged even when lessons were creative and active. The idea of having to recite large amounts of information to them without books . . . yikes!

In fact, while it took centuries for educators to really digest it, the book's true power was that it allowed teachers to reimagine their role. It meant that teachers were no longer simply dispensers of knowledge; they could become explainers, mentors, and facilitators. We talk a lot about "flipped" classrooms today, so I'll put it this way: the book first "flipped" the classroom more than five centuries ago.

Of course, simply having books doesn't guarantee a thing. It took centuries to really appreciate how books could change instruction. And even after all these centuries, there are too many classrooms where students sit hunched reading dreary texts or where teachers spend whole classes parroting things students have already read. As with any other technology, the presence of a book matters less than how good it is and how well it's used.

The book provides an invaluable template for how to think about education technology. The book has been singularly impactful in schooling for a simple reason: it's changed what teachers do and how students learn. Understanding the book's strengths and limitations can help illuminate the promise of newer technologies.

For instance, students learn best when their eyes and ears are working in tandem, but books are a silent medium. Books are fixed, providing the same experience to every reader, every time. The material and language in any book will inevitably be too difficult for some readers and too easy for others. Books can't offer a live demonstration or an alternative explanation to a confused reader.

Online materials, on the other hand, can be rapidly updated. They are customizable to a student's interests and reading level. They feature embedded exercises that let students apply new concepts and get immediate feedback. Virtual instruction makes it possible for students to access real, live teachers from any location, allowing students to see them, listen to them, and talk to them—not just see their words on the page.

If students need additional assistance, computer-assisted tutoring might help. If students need access to courses not available at their school, virtual instruction might.

Technology can be a powerful lever for rethinking schools and systems. But the rethinking is more important than the technology. TNT was originally invented in 1863 by a German chemist for use as a yellow dye. Forty years later, people realized it could also be an explosive. A new technology is not innately "good" or "bad." What matters is what we do with it.

So what's the right way to think about education technology? It's by starting with learning challenges. Schools have trouble giving struggling students or English language learners enough individualized attention. They have trouble challenging gifted children. More daily personalized support and practice are always in demand. The thing is, most schools don't have the staff to make that feasible. What to do?

Technology can help. Kurt VanLehn, a professor of computer science at Arizona State University, has reviewed scores of studies examining "intelligent" computer-based tutoring systems and found that the best ones nearly match the performance of human tutors. These systems provide targeted feedback and repeated practice, adjust the pace to the individual student, use a variety of illustrations and explanations, and employ both audio and visual cues. They don't get tired or sick, never have a bad day, and can offer a detailed picture of how students are doing.

Computer-based tutoring may be a promising way to provide more students with more individualized support. That's it. But that's enough. It won't replace teachers or "flip" schools. What it will do is provide students with much-needed support and allow teachers to spend less time on routinized drills. Come to think of it, that seems like plenty.

When I talk to the leaders of schools or systems heralded for their success with technology, it's striking how consistently they brush past the tech in order to talk about learning, people, problem-solving, and redesign. That's why they're successful. That's the right way to think about technology. It's not about hardware, software, or cool gizmos—it's about finding ways to give students the opportunities, time, attention, and support they need.

All of this is easily lost when enthusiasts promise that technology will (finally) "revolutionize" schools and skeptics respond that it's all an "attack on teachers." That kind of bombast is a distraction. After all, the book didn't work miracles or replace teachers. What it did was give us the opportunity to reimagine teaching and learning, even if we're still struggling to capitalize on it five centuries hence.

15

Philanthropy and
Its Discontents

IN 2010, FACEBOOK FOUNDER Mark Zuckerberg went on *The Oprah Winfrey Show* to announce he was giving $100 million to public education in Newark, New Jersey. Hurriedly arranged, partly to take the edge off a biting portrayal of Zuckerberg in a new movie on the birth of Facebook, the gift was the largest ever granted to a single school district. It was even bigger than it seemed, since Newark's leadership committed to matching it by raising an additional $100 million.

Sounds like a ton of money, doesn't it? Well, the $200 million was paid out over four years, so it came out to $50 million a year. Newark was already spending around $1 billion a year even before Zuckerberg's gift. So the gift amounted only to a temporary 5 percent bump in district spending. Put that way, it seems odd to imagine that the gift might transform one of the nation's most troubled school districts. (That's a funny thing about public education: we already spend so much that even enormous figures can get swallowed up.) The hope, though, was that the gift would spark the energy and political wherewithal to fuel system change.

As the payments were ending, I penned a fairly acerbic assessment of the lessons learned. I said the effort had been hasty and hobbled by miscalculation.[1] I soon heard from a number of irate callers. As one told me, "You've got this all wrong. We developed a strong plan and executed it. There's a great new teachers' contract. There were a few bumps, but that's natural. Any fair person would say we've had a lot of success."

That's one take. Reporter Dale Russakoff summed things up differently in her celebrated 2015 book *The Prize*. She observed that the effort got off to a slow start, struggled with Newark's administrative bloat, spent heavily on consultants, and encountered fierce community resistance. The hard-charging superintendent who led the reform effort was pushed out. Newark mayor Cory Booker moved on to the US Senate and was succeeded by the most prominent opponent of the reforms.

It can be tricky to objectively evaluate how an ambitious reform fared, even in hindsight. My intent isn't to judge Zuckerberg or Newark. What I find striking, though, is how easy it is for donors and their grantees to reflexively regard criticism as unfounded or off-base.

Ultimately, donors and foundation staff don't have to answer to anybody besides themselves. They're free to interpret their experiences however they like. This is why they can come across as unaccountable and smitten with their own wisdom. But let's keep things in perspective. If you're bitterly angry at someone who's voluntarily giving away large sums of money, you probably need to take a deep breath. Generosity is a good thing. And spending money to influence policy—whether to promote charter schools, protect wildlife, or raise the minimum wage—is wholly in the American tradition of free speech and pluralism.

All that said, it's as unhelpful to lionize education funders as it is to vilify them. I've been writing about philanthropy for nearly two decades. Back in 2005, I tackled it in my book *With the Best of Intentions: How Philanthropy is Reshaping K–12 Education*. At that time, only a tiny sliver of media coverage on education giving was critical, while a healthy chunk offered fawning profiles of donors or programs. Serious explorations of the subject were few and far between.[2]

As a jumping-off point for the book, I used the most famous instance of 1990s education giving: the $1.1 billion Annenberg Challenge. At a 1994 White House ceremony, Ambassador Walter Annenberg announced a $500 million gift to K–12 schooling. It was the biggest gift ever made to K–12 education. Augmented by $600 million in matching funds, Annenberg sought to spur bottom-up reform in select urban and rural communities. The results were dismal. The money got frittered away, the effort got bogged down in endless community conversations and small initiatives, and the end result yielded little meaningful or lasting change. The veteran chief at the Council of Great City Schools famously concluded that the lesson was, "Don't do that again."[3]

Things started to change in the late 1990s and early 2000s, as a new generation of philanthropists—with names like Gates, Walton, Dell, Broad, and Fischer—entered K–12. They shared an impatience, an entrepreneurial bent, and a focus on measured outcomes that set them apart from established givers. They embraced charter schooling and policy change. And, for better or worse, they have played an enormous role in shaping big-*R* Reform.

They've done much that has been good and promising. A decade ago, funders fumed that investments in nifty practices never seemed to deliver lasting improvement and that successful programs and models never seemed to grow successfully. The new funders grasped these challenges and began to tackle system rigidity, leadership, and policy.

In doing so, they were guided by three insights. First, they internalized the lesson taught by University of Arkansas professor Jay Greene, who pointed out in *Best of Intentions* that education philanthropy is so small relative to K–12 schooling—amounting to less than 1 percent of spending—that investments will make a big impact only if "leveraged" to drive policy change.[4] Second, they learned that research and advocacy were important tools for influencing policy and began to strategize accordingly. Third, they realized that their funds might be only a drop in the bucket, but could still have an outsized impact because so much school spending is already tied up in salaries, benefits, and buildings.

There's a lot to like here. The new philanthropy has helped break the grip of school districts, textbook companies, and education schools by offering footholds to those who would otherwise be boxed out. Donors provide funds to support new voices; make the case for alternative policies; and nurture, launch, and grow promising ventures. This is all consistent with philanthropy's vital place in America's decentralized, pluralist fabric.

At the same time, the nature of the new education philanthropy means foundations can exercise a disconcerting degree of influence. I've mentioned previously that, while at the University of Virginia, I explored how school systems in Milwaukee, Cleveland, and Edgewood (Texas) responded to school vouchers. I could do that research only because a foundation provided the funds to pay for regular air travel, rental cars, motel rooms, loads of fast food, interview transcripts, and research assistants. Given my generally positive view of school choice, the foundation's staff anticipated that I'd find it was forcing these systems to improve.

After two years and hundreds of interviews, I wrote a book concluding that the story was much more complicated. (If you're curious, it's called *Revolution at the Margins*.)[5] Choice could yield systemic benefits but, for some interesting reasons, hadn't thus far. Because it was at odds with the funder's hopes and views, that conclusion was a real loser for me. Don't get me wrong. The funder never threatened me or tried to dictate my findings, and I'd hoped the foundation staff might regard my work as instructive. But they deemed the results a disappointment, with the less said about them, the better.

I'd like to say that my efforts were rewarded. But that's not how it works. Foundations operate a lot like Santa Claus, with goodies to give away and a careful eye on who's been naughty and who's been nice. I wound up on the naughty list, I fear, and never heard from that foundation again. On one level, that's no big deal. It's their money and they're free (and should be free!) to fund whomever they like. On another level, though, it is a big deal; it means that philanthropy can erode honesty and independence—even when nobody intends it to.

It's funny how foundation officials simultaneously manage to acknowledge and dismiss concerns about all this. They tell you that they know people are sucking up to them and, to demonstrate that they get it, they all tell the same self-deprecating jokes. (The most common one, which I've heard countless times, is, "When I took this job, X told me, 'You'll never again have a bad meal or a bad idea.' And X was right!")

Of course, because the joke-teller might be giving away big chunks of cash, we all roar as if it's the funniest thing we've ever heard. That's the problem. Foundation staff get treated with kid gloves. They're always welcome. Everyone nods in appreciation when they speak. Even their dumbest statements are greeted with, "That's really insightful and important. Let me just add . . . " Smart, accomplished people jump through hoops to meet with them or respond to their requests. When foundation staff fail to honor commitments or promises, hardly anyone is inclined to call them on it. Could you live like that and not wind up with an inflated sense of your place in the world? I sure couldn't.

Insulated by that cocoon of niceness, funders tend to fall into some unfortunate habits (no matter how many self-deprecating jokes they tell). They steer conversations toward their current strategy, because that's what's relevant and useful in the moment. When conversation strays too far from their agenda, their eyes glaze over and they tune out things they ought to hear. Most longtime reformers have had the eerie experience of repeatedly making point x to a foundation official over months or years, having it ignored, and then having the official later ask, "Have you ever thought about point x?" and say that they wish someone had brought it up earlier. Sigh.

Most foundation staff spend a *lot* of time talking to people they fund, people they might fund, or people trying to woo them. They spend every day talking about their vision and mission, how to refine it, and how to execute it, and they do this mostly with people who want their money. Given all that, it's easy to wind up in a self-assured, mission-driven bubble. After enough of this, almost any unsolicited critique can seem misinformed or unfair, and taken as proof that the critic "just doesn't get it."

I know it sounds like I'm being hard on foundation staff. I don't mean it that way. Their roles can be exhausting. There are lots of personal politics: they need to stay in tune with colleagues, the foundation's strategy, and the preferences of the donor or the board. At any large foundation, they need to keep pushing large sums out the door just to comply with tax regulations (this can require giving away millions every week). They have to spend long days writing and reading reports about their grantees. Their jobs can require lots of travel and loads of meetings. They have to tread carefully around prohibitions on political involvement. They have to speak cautiously, as offhand remarks might be taken as official statements of foundation policy. I think of the friend who told me, "I always thought foundation jobs were a pretty sweet deal. Then I took this one. It's frustrating, it's tedious, and it's kicking my ass."

And most funders do take self-appraisal seriously. They evaluate grants, interview grantees, and convene groups to offer feedback. This is all swell, until they feel like they've heard all the arguments and sorted through all the options. The thing is: they haven't. Even the toughest-minded, thickest-skinned friends tend to tread gently when they are disagreeing with a funder or they fear they may be saying something that the funder doesn't want to hear.

That's why prickly, even hostile, scrutiny is so healthy. Skeptics can raise the unpleasant issues and ask the annoying questions that friends typically won't. But effective critics must also exhibit self-control and engage constructively. Unfortunately, not enough actually do.

You see the problem. When criticized harshly, funders get defensive. In turn, critics get irritated and increasingly nasty, prompting funders to tune them out even more firmly. Then critics complain that funders don't listen to them, and around and around we go.

Foundation staff can be hard of hearing, but reformers are also guilty of failing to speak up. After all, funders play a big role in making projects, programs, and research possible—even impacting job security and career prospects. So why risk alienating them if you don't have to? Even if they're in a position to be impolitic, reformers still work with districts, researchers, and colleagues who want foundation dollars. Incurring the wrath of a donor can make one less attractive to skittish partners. All of this fosters an amiable conspiracy of silence.

There are also times when foundations start to feel uncomfortably pushy and when all the talk of "mission alignment" can be taken to mean, "If you want money, get with the program." I remember one call from a colleague at a left-leaning think tank in 2012 or so. He told me that a New York funder wanted us to host joint dialogues on the Common Core for Washington officials and media. It sounded like a good idea.

The funder wanted the first session to feature Jeb Bush, former governor of Florida and the most prominent Republican supporter of the Common Core. I said, "Sure," but commented that we'd want a prominent critic for the next session, in the spirit of balance and robust debate. He said, "Makes sense. Let me see what they think." I didn't hear from him for weeks. Finally, my friend called back and explained, "Your idea won't fly. It wasn't what they had in mind." What they wanted, it turned out, was a series of events plugging the Common Core. If I'd signed on, I'd have attracted big bucks and built a relationship with a new funder. Because I didn't, it was, "See ya!"

These issues get much more troubling when foundations partner with the federal government, as has happened with initiatives like Race to the Top and the Investing in Innovation (i3) fund. Foundations helped underwrite state applications and preparation sessions for Race to the Top and provided matching funds for i3 winners. When foundations and the federal government link arms, disagreeing with the president's policies becomes tantamount to attacking the foundation's agenda—and vice versa. Rather than sparking exploration and debate, that's a recipe for shutting it down.

I wish I knew what to do about any of this, other than encourage funders to think of their own work more in terms of "little-*p*" rather than "big-*P*" philanthropy—that is, with more emphasis on rethinking and less on the agenda of the moment. Lacking good answers, I'll close instead with a couple of reflections.

One thing that critics resent is a foundation's ability to move on when things don't work out. Funders get excited about things like small high schools, education technology, or a local teacher pay initiative and they dive in. Later, when they conclude the old strategy isn't working or just decide to change direction, it's easy for them to move on while educators and communities deal with the aftermath. That's natural and probably inevitable, but funders would do well to think and talk more explicitly about how their decisions affect the people left behind. This takes on special resonance when funders choose to get involved in policy or governance and not just the giving away of school supplies.

Critics also have a point when they complain about the lack of accountability for funders and staff. When foundations aggressively push their agendas, it can feel to those in schools and systems like outsiders are foisting change on them. If programs or policies disappoint, it's not clear whether those outsiders are ever held accountable. This feels especially off to observers who routinely hear funders talk about the importance of holding schools and educators accountable for *their* performance.

It takes money to do things. Programs, staff, research, advocacy, and pretty much everything else that happens in school reform requires funding. This gives funders oceans of influence. Yet this influence is accompanied by behaviors that rarely get examined or discussed. Reformers should change that. They should talk openly about the influence of funders and expect that foundations be at least as answerable for their actions as they'd like educators to be.

16

Beware the Media Glare

REPORTERS HAVE IT ROUGH. I know. Back in college, my first summer job was working as a general assignment reporter for *Florida Today*. All kinds of stories were thrown at me: mysterious pelican deaths, Cape Canaveral glitches, police blotter wrap-ups, you name it.

The one I recall most vividly, though, is when a young man was murdered in a beaten-down housing project. My job was to go door-to-door and get quotes from neighbors who'd just seen a body carried away. Talk about feeling ghoulish. During a night spent that way, you find that most people have no desire to talk to you and that there's something off-putting about those who do. That was the night I decided journalism was too grueling for me.

There was a reason that my paper wanted those quotes, though. The press stays in business by attracting viewers and readers. That's why it's drawn to violent crime. Generally speaking, the press favors stories that offer drama, conflict, and strong personalities. Grand plans and bold declarations play well; nuance and complexity, not so much.

I once chatted with the *New York Times* education reporter for a story on whether foundation support compromised the independence of advocates and researchers. My reward? He quoted me on page 1 saying, "We're all indicted" for taking Gates funding. Umm . . . I had actually said that everyone involved in education seeks funds from somewhere, so "we're all indicted" in this process. That would have made for a pretty dull story, though.

The media also has a short attention span. It's in the news business; it's drawn to new things. Incremental changes can be a tough sell, particularly when they're complicated.

The media's appetites can cause problems if reformers allow them to shape their thinking. Judging what's important based on what attracts press interest can distort the judgment of even smart, strategic reformers. It can lead reformers to emphasize what's shallow and saleable. Here, I want to chat a bit about three cases that I find especially instructive on all this.

The first was the long wait for the movie *Waiting for Superman*,[1] and the underwhelming results when it finally arrived. In the years preceding the 2010 documentary, at every convening of education reformers someone would inevitably declare, "We need our own *Inconvenient Truth*! That'll wake people up. *That's* the game-changer we need!" *An Inconvenient Truth* was the 2006 Academy Award–winning documentary that sparked heightened attention to global warming. It was widely credited with helping to build political momentum for the cause.

I have a clear memory of one public relations pro pitching a foundation officer, explaining the need to spend more on mass media while name-checking *An Inconvenient Truth*. The PR pro said, "The people you're trying to reach aren't interested in articles or arguments. You need to make things simpler, stupider, and snazzier." That was a mantra at the time: big-R Reforms like charter schooling were suffering because their champions were too thoughtful for their own good. Hollywood movies seemed like the perfect antidote.

When *Waiting for Superman* came out, anticipation was high. Reformers were ecstatic. A good friend, a school reform veteran of several decades, attended an early screening where a famed newspaper columnist whispered to him, "I guess this makes all your work worth it." (My friend reported feeling vaguely ill at this view of his efforts.)

And then . . . the movie pretty much came and went. Even with $2 million in promotional backing from the Gates Foundation, enthusiastic and organized support from school reformers, and an aggressive media campaign, *Superman's* box office haul lagged behind that of two other 2010 documentaries (*Babies* and *Oceans*).

For all the excited chatter about the movie, it was hard to find any discernible impact. What went wrong? Well, one problem was the notion that reformers' big challenge was "messaging." Here's the thing: any time you're trying to win a public debate that affects other people's kids, your first response to resistance shouldn't be "more messaging." It should be to ask why people aren't embracing your ideas. When someone says the problem is "messaging," what they really mean is, "We're right. The problem is that that Americans are just too dumb to understand that we're right." Maybe. But I'm not sold.

In his TV and radio appearances, *Superman*'s director Davis Guggenheim offered a cringeworthy mix of hubris and banality. He insisted, "In recent years, we've cracked the code. The high-performing charter schools, like KIPP and others, have figured out the system that works for kids in even the toughest neighborhoods." Guggenheim explained that school reform was simple: "The solution is great teachers. The high-performing charters have great teachers."[2] This is what messaging sounds like.

Messaging isn't a magical formula for change. Even if you're good at manipulating emotions, it turns out that it's really difficult to turn vague notions of "we need to do something" into meaningful reform. Worse, the movie's "action steps" included stuff like sending a text message or attending a school board meeting. The takeaways offered viewers nothing concrete, substantive, or obviously beneficial for their kids. Here's a rule of thumb: *If you don't give people anything to do, they won't do anything.* Worse still, messaging distracts reformers from practical questions like, "Exactly what solution are we offering?" and, "Why aren't people excited about it?"

A focus on messaging elevates simple but silly claims—like the notion that we've "cracked the code" or that good charters are all filled with "great teachers." It usually comes at the expense of listening to concerns or doing a better job of explaining how favored reforms will actually help kids. The reformers eagerly waiting for *Waiting for Superman* didn't do those things. Instead, they hoped that better messaging would suffice. This is a mistake made time and again. When *Waiting for Superman* yielded disappointing results, more than a few reformers quickly concluded that what reformers needed was . . . yep, even more messaging.

How Michelle Rhee got turned into a caricature is the story of a different kind of media-induced distortion. In 2007, Rhee became chancellor of the District of Columbia Public Schools (DCPS). Rhee had enjoyed enormous success as founder of The New Teacher Project, a Teach For America spin-off. I'd said over the years that I thought she'd make an intriguing superintendent because she was strategic, fearless, and a master of the critical back-office district operations that few really understand. At DCPS, Rhee took off at a sprint, tackling a special education system wracked by legal troubles and wasteful spending, a broken textbook distribution system, and central office dysfunction. She implemented a pioneering teacher evaluation system and a transformative collective bargaining agreement. It was impressive as hell.

Along the way, Rhee made plenty of enemies. She was frustrated that she had few allies to help make her case or answer the Washington Teachers Union's furious attacks. She told me that local parents and professionals were offering to help, but "I don't have anyone to take their names or coordinate them." Rhee saw her lack of advocates as a big problem, one that forced her to rely more on the bully pulpit than she'd have liked.

Things came to a head in late 2008 when Rhee appeared on the cover of *Time* magazine, grim-faced and holding a broom, alongside the headline "How to Fix America's Schools." The magazine photo shoot had been mostly warm and fuzzy shots of her posing with students. Then, at the last minute, the photographer suggested the picture with the broom. And that was the picture that showed up on the cover. A lot of advocates, funders, and political types loved the photo, but the picture helped turn Rhee into a caricature. She knew it, too.

That cover helped etch a combative, bombastic image of Rhee in the public mind. While most observers thought that she had spurred dramatic, positive change in DCPS, her controversial profile overshadowed all of that. In 2010, after her boss, DC mayor Adrian Fenty, lost his reelection bid, Rhee stepped down and launched the advocacy group StudentsFirst. She wanted to provide other state and local education leaders with the allies and advocacy she'd lacked in Washington. With her smarts and hard-won experience, she could have been great at it. But the media wanted the circus.

They wanted incendiary TV appearances and scathing quotes. That media attention gave Rhee visibility, which is like catnip to advocates and funders.

The more Rhee played along, the farther she got from what had made her effective in the first place. In the short term, funders, talking heads, and advocates reward you for being colorful. As the novelty wears off, though, staying relevant requires being more and more outrageous. After a while, you drift into caricature, and then everyone moves on to a fresh face. Eventually, Rhee handed off StudentsFirst and largely left school reform behind. It can be tempting to give the crowd what they want, but the price is often exacting.

A third illustration of the perils of the press's enthusiasms is the tale of how the *Los Angeles Times* helped turn a useful statistical exercise into the poster child for the "war on teachers." Over the past decade, one of the more bizarre developments in education has been the notion that asking teachers to be accountable professionals constitutes a war on teachers. At least, it would be bizarre, if not for a wave of half-baked teacher accountability systems and the accompanying rhetoric that professionals in any field would find galling.

In summer 2010, to the uproarious cheers of big-*R* Reformers, the *Times* ran a multipart, front-page series analyzing teacher value-added scores in the Los Angeles Unified School District (LAUSD).[3] The paper used seven years of reading and math scores to calculate performance for third-through fifth-grade teachers and then published each teacher's results online. I'm all for transparency, and I think value-added measures can be a useful tool for thinking about how schools, systems, and educators are doing. But, as I wrote at the time, what the *Times* did "puts more stress on primitive systems than they can bear, and promises to unnecessarily entangle a useful management tool in personalities and public reputations."[4]

The analysis downplayed concerns about the validity and reliability of the test scores, and about the fact that the results bounced around significantly based on which statistical models were used. It ignored the extent to which a teacher's results might have been directly affected by the work of colleagues who taught their students, as in the case of students who received special education or pull-out instruction.

More importantly, the exercise failed to distinguish between responsible oversight and public titillation. Public oversight doesn't entail reporting how many traffic citations individual police officers issue or what score a National Guardsman receives on her performance review. Why? Because these data are inevitably imperfect, using them sensibly requires judgment, and such judgment becomes difficult when decisions are made in the public eye.

The *LA Times* took a reasonable intuition, overextended it, and turned it into something that teachers justifiably perceived as a hatchet job. The result turned a potentially promising small-*r* reform into a big-*R* crusade.

Those of us who saw merit in value-added analysis but disliked what the *Times* had done got grief from big-*R* Reformers for saying so. As one longtime friend asked me, "Rick, are you trying to score points with the unions or are you just going squishy?" When I said, "Come on, I've said a million times that what matters is *how* we use something like value-added, not just *whether* we use it," he just shook his head. It was as if being a *real* reformer requires taking promising ideas and then pushing them past their breaking point.

Rather than the smashing victory for big-*R* Reform that some had initially envisioned, the *Times'* display helped make value-added radioactive. Previously, the president of the American Federation of Teachers had gingerly expressed openness to value-added measures, even penning a foreword for a book about them. Before long, though, she was denouncing value-added metrics (VAM) and insisting, "VAM is a sham!" The *Times'* exercise became a symbol of how value-added measures could be abused, and contributed to a shift in which value-added would be seen less and less as a potentially promising tool and more and more as a controversial weapon that teachers should regard with fear and loathing.

The media has an uncommon ability to play havoc with school reform. It can prompt reformers to think like salesmen. It can turn people into caricatures and even get them to cooperate in the process. It can bend promising ideas into a media-friendly muddle. That's just the nature of the beast. Be forewarned.

The first time I ever sat with a media coach, I could see the pity in her eyes. I talked too fast, went on too long, jumbled my points, waved my hands wildly . . . I was a mess. Seeing that there was too much to fix at once, she kept it simple. "Rick, two things to remember," she said. "One, if you're on TV, look at the camera, smile, and remember that you're the expert. Two, whether it's print or TV, keep it simple, sharp, and short." That's good advice. But it's also a reminder that what plays well in the media doesn't necessarily have a lot to do with nuance, thoughtfulness, or reflection.

The spotlight can be distracting. Here are three simple rules I've learned over the years that might help keep things in perspective. The press isn't your enemy, but it's also not your friend. The point of reform is not to get quoted or featured in a documentary. And, finally, don't let what reporters find appealing dictate what you deem important.

17

School Reform Left and Right

I'M A CONSERVATIVE. In the world of school reform, this makes me something of an outlier.

Now, you may not believe that I'm an outlier. After all, you may have heard charter school advocates, Teach For America (TFA), and even *Democrats* (!) for Education Reform blasted as "right-wing, neoliberal corporatizers." I'll let you in on a secret: they're not. Most of them are Democrats and progressives who voted for Barack Obama and Hillary Clinton, support active government, and lean to the left on social issues.

In fact, my estimate has long been that 90 percent of big-*R* Reformers are progressives. If you doubt that figure, survey the next fifty TFA alums, foundation staff, and education advocates you bump into. I'd be surprised if more than one in ten voted for a Republican president in the past decade, wants to cut welfare programs, opposes race-based affirmative action, or belongs to the National Rifle Association.

If you think someone who supports welfare spending, affirmative action, and gun control is "right-wing" just because they like charter schooling, you might want to check with some local Republicans. A fondness for charter schools may mark someone as right-leaning in education, but in the larger world, I've just described a good chunk of the nation's Democratic officeholders. The fact that progressives who like charter schools can get attacked as "right-wing" mostly goes to show that the center of gravity in schooling sits pretty far to the left of where it does for most of America.

This imbalance matters because progressives and conservatives think about policy differently. Progressives tend to see social policy in terms of structural inequities—particularly race, class, and gender. Conservatives are more prone to see things in terms of individual responsibility.

Of course, most people instinctively grasp that it's always about both. Crime, poverty, unemployment, and educational success are products of both structural forces and individual choices. And I've yet to meet a conservative education reformer who denies the role of structural inequities or a progressive reformer who says that personal responsibility doesn't matter.

In many ways, education is uniquely suited for ideological cooperation, as it offers a way to both combat structural inequities and cultivate personal responsibility. Education can open the doors of opportunity and provide all students with a more equitable start. These are things that those on the right and left both want.

Moreover, when it comes to the stuff of schooling, progressives and conservatives agree on a lot. We all want every child to attend schools that fire their imaginations, impart knowledge, teach critical skills, equip them to be responsible citizens, inspire joy, and prepare them for success. The disagreements are usually over how to do all this.

Thus it's no surprise that, for decades, education reformers on the left and right found lots of opportunity to work together. The bipartisan reform agenda included expanding school choice, overhauling teacher tenure and pay, making schooling more rigorous and accountable, supporting research and data collection, and revamping teacher preparation.

Over time, that consensus has started to fracture. When it comes to school reform, there are fault lines where those on the left and right, *in good faith*, can deeply and fundamentally disagree.

Here's one small example: I was helping a district host a community meeting on student discipline. As in most places, the district was disciplining black and Latino students at a much higher rate than white or Asian students. Shown the data, one local minister slammed his fist on the table and bellowed, "This is unacceptable! This is nothing but old-fashioned racism, whether the teachers mean it to be or not. Those numbers need to come down—now!"

Another attendee responded, "Hold on! If some kids are causing more trouble, they *should* be getting suspended more. You all should figure that out before you start giving anyone a free pass." This is the kind of tension that arises between those focused on addressing inequities and those worried about undermining notions of personal responsibility. Who was right? Well, I think they both had a point—and the best solutions are informed by that.

While much of what left and right disagree on may be the particulars rather than the big picture, those differences can be critical. That's particularly true when it comes to big questions like race-conscious measures and the proper role of social policy.

I've yet to meet anyone in school reform, for instance, who wouldn't like schools to have more racially diverse teachers and leaders. Many on the left think race-conscious remedies are needed to overcome structural inequities and deeply ingrained patterns of thought. They see a need for role models and mentors and view reservations about race-conscious hiring as thinly veiled excuses for racism. Conservatives, on the other hand, may sympathize with the goal but worry when attention to group identification seems to overshadow considerations of character or merit. They fear that race-conscious policies will institutionalize division, resentment, and grievance.

When it comes to social policy, progressives are inclined to think that experts can devise policies and programs that will help address society's ills. They believe that government intervention is essential to promote progress and equity, and that the government needs to correct for problems caused by structural forces, self-interested corporations, or individual misfortune. In schooling, they see the federal government as the indispensable guardian of vulnerable children.

Conservatives have less faith in the power of government to solve problems. They believe social progress tends to be incremental and the product of local communities, private associations, and dynamic markets. Fearing that social engineering frequently causes more problems than it solves, conservatives are inclined to think that government solutions do more to promote compliance, paperwork, and bureaucracy than to improve schools.

These philosophical divides are married to practical differences in how those on the right and left live and in what they value. The Pew Research Center reported in 2014 that 77 percent of liberals would prefer to live in a community where "the houses are smaller and closer to each other, but schools, stores and restaurants are within walking distance," while 75 percent of conservatives would prefer bigger houses even if communities were less walkable. Seventy-six percent of liberals deem racial and ethnic diversity important in deciding where to live, compared with 20 percent of conservatives. And just 17 percent of liberals, compared with 57 percent of conservatives, think that having their religious faith well represented in a community is important.[1]

Conservatives may make up about half the country, but they're a distinct minority in school reform circles today. One can survey the major education philanthropies and advocacy groups and only rarely find an actual right-winger. This creates blind spots. I've been struck, for instance, by how many big-*R* Reformers gradually incorporated specific, left-leaning stances on immigration, policing, campus protests, and gender identity into their agendas and talking points—all the while seeming to assume that this wouldn't impact their efforts to work with conservatives or Republican legislators in the states. They were wrong.

The shame of it is that principled bipartisanship has a critical role to play in school reform. That's because schooling is a complex, personal enterprise in which it matters immensely whether parents in a given community trust reformers and how reform is pursued.

If improving schools were like fighting to abolish the death penalty—where victory is cut-and-dried—then bipartisanship would matter less. Advocates could just worry about winning votes or swaying judges. After all, if the death penalty is abolished, that's it. One side wins. Story over. But school reform is different. It's not enough for school reformers to win a policy fight; they need the kind of broad support that sustains change. The success of school reform rests on thousands of actions taken by educators, community leaders, and officials in schools, systems, and states. Because America is a quilt of red and blue communities, success requires support from both camps.

Does this seem like a tall order? If so, it may help to keep in mind that, as University of Southern California psychology professor Jesse Graham and a couple of his colleagues have observed, "The ideological 'culture war' in the U.S. is, in part, an honest disagreement about ends . . . But our findings suggest that there is an additional process at work: partisans on each side exaggerate the degree to which the other side pursues moral ends that are different from their own. Much of this exaggeration comes from each side underestimating the degree to which the other side shares its own values."[2]

Honest, constructive debate between right and left makes for smarter decisions about policy and practice. Progressives and conservatives see the world in different ways, sometimes want different things, and favor different kinds of solutions. This is extraordinarily healthy, especially when we also make it a point to recall the values and aspirations that unite us. In the end, progressives and conservatives need each other. They're two sides of a single coin.

18

What Parenthood Taught Me About School Reform

I'D BEEN A SCHOOL REFORMER for close to two decades before I became a dad. This gave me the luxury of emotional distance; I didn't have to square what I was championing with my own children's experiences. I'd always wondered how that might change when I had kids of my own.

Over the years, some friends had told me that having kids had made them more impassioned in their commitment to big-*R* Reform. Others quietly admitted to being torn, that their professional focus on test-based accountability coexisted uneasily with their desire to see their own kids in warm, arts-laden schools.

That's natural. We all respond differently to individuals than to groups or abstractions. That's why firsthand accounts hit us so hard—they make things personal. As a teacher, I got emotional about my students but never felt that same attachment to the hundreds of other kids roaming our hallways.

Well, parenthood affected me like it affects most people: it knocked my world off its axis. I never loved anyone like I love my boys. And I'd never been as frustrated by anyone or anything. It's that exhaustion and emotional investment that make our kids so dear to us, I think. Parents know the countless times they've reminded their kid to say "Thank you." They remember those long nights sitting on the bathroom floor with a sick, screaming kid. There's nothing intellectual about the bond. It's primal. And it changes us in fundamental ways.

When our first son, Grayson, was born, I became more patient. Where I used to sweat over five wasted minutes, I now found myself okay with gobs of wasted time. It made me more empathetic. I used to be one of those travelers who'd grit their teeth when little kids shrieked and babbled on airplanes. After Gray, I stopped minding. Parenthood rewrote my schedule and routines. It made me want to hustle home every night for dinner and bedtime, pretty much putting an end to my after-work socializing. It made me kinder.

When it came to school reform, though, in important ways, parenthood didn't affect my thinking at all. I still thought that good educators should be paid more than bad ones, that policy is a limited tool, and that it's a mistake to treat reading and math achievement as a proxy for school quality. I still thought that the appealing, generous thing about school reform is the promise that we can do better by every child.

I did, however, find that some things struck me with new force, including how little the big-*R* Reform agenda had to say to me as a parent. Proposals designed for dysfunctional urban systems seemed mostly irrelevant to my parental concerns. Talk of accountability and charter schooling focused almost entirely on raising reading and math scores for children in poverty. Concerns that curricula had been narrowed or that schools were shortchanging gifted students were dismissed by big-*R* Reformers as exaggerated or ill-founded.

As a parent, I found myself less interested than ever in whether someone's analysis purported to show that a given reform might boost the nation's gross domestic product a half century hence. I was far more inclined to ask whether a given proposal seemed likely to improve *my* kids' schools. I suspect that I'm hardly unique in making that calculation.

Parenthood left me attuned to how frequently reformers can get downright dismissive when it comes to kids who aren't minorities and aren't in poverty. I recall the friend who allowed during a break from a contentious meeting that she wouldn't mind seeing "some of those comfortable little darlings learn what it's like to be homeless and unemployed." More typically, bland assurances that white, suburban kids (like mine) "will be fine" seemed to me to betray the premise of reform—that schools can and should do better for *all* children.

As a parent, I have one job above all others: watching out for my kids. Even when advocates passionately claim to have my kids' best interests at heart, I think I'd be a pretty lousy father if I allowed their judgment to trump my own. There was an iconic congressional exchange that put a fine point on this. As Senator Christopher Bond, a Republican from Missouri, recalled it, "A couple of years ago, one of my colleagues . . . was in a debate with a representative in the Department of Education. The Department of Education person said, 'I care just as much about your children and their success as you do.' To which [my colleague] replied, 'Well, that's great. Do you know their names?'"[1]

Big-R Reformers know all this at a gut level. And I've known plenty of equity-inflamed reformers who've gone to great lengths to make sure their own children attend great schools and colleges—abstractions be damned. They spring for tutoring, finagle private school admissions, and pull every lever they can find.

Yet, swept up in their passions, too many big-R Reformers have developed the unfortunate habit of denouncing parents who worry overmuch about what a given reform means for *their* kids. The vitriol has been directed at suburban parents and parents in cities like New Orleans and Newark who voice doubts about charter schools, mayoral control, or the Common Core. Time and again, I've heard concerned parents described not as admirably involved or as potential allies, but as problems to be overcome.

The idea that parents deserve a respectful hearing really shouldn't be that hard to fathom. Reformers and parents both want better schools—they just see things from different perspectives. Reformers are necessarily dealing with children in mass batches. That's the nature of system reform. Parents don't see things that way.

Big-R Reformers tend to talk as if opposition is evidence that parents are selfish or unwilling to do "what's right for kids." This phrasing quickly poisons honest disagreements. After all, if you're "for the kids" and I disagree with you, then you must think that I'm "*against* the kids."

The thing to remember is that all parents are for *their* kids. Now, some parents may sometimes want things for their kids that you think are bad for other kids—or even for their own. Fair enough. If your reform strategy is at odds with what lots of parents want for their kids, though, it's worth reflecting on why that is. It's possible that it's about more than their being obtuse or uncaring.

Take the "opt-out" movement that's emerged in recent years, partly in response to Common Core tests that can stretch eight hours or more. By 2016, more than one in five New York students was refusing to take the state test. In some of New York's school systems, over half the students were. Opt-out parents complained that the tests were poorly designed, were too long, didn't provide useful information to parents or teachers, and wouldn't improve instruction.

Big-*R* Reformers countered that the new tests would help hold schools accountable and give parents a reality check on how students were doing in school. Stand for Children cofounder Jonah Edelman told the compelling story of a Memphis grandmother who "was horrified to discover after we taught her how to interpret standardized test results that her four grandchildren—*all* of whom were getting As and Bs in school—were up to *three* grades behind in reading."[2]

Reformers made valid, important points, but didn't seem interested in understanding parental concerns, much less in addressing them. They routinely dismissed opt-out parents as irresponsible and misinformed. Merryl Tisch, chancellor of New York's Board of Regents, thundered, "Those who call for 'opting out' really want New York to 'opt out' of information that can help parents and teachers understand how well students are doing . . . It's time to stop making noise to protect the adults and start speaking up for the students."[3]

Instead of suggesting that opt-out parents aren't for the students, big-*R* Reformers could have tried a lot harder to grasp why parents thought these tests were bad for their kids. Here's what I mean: Reformers sometimes trot out an instructive analogy to answer opt-outers. They point out that few parents object to taking their child to the pediatrician for a check-up. These school tests are just another kind of check-up, they note, so what's the problem?

It's a good analogy. But thinking like a parent should also help big-*R* Reformers see where it breaks down. It's true that parents generally don't mind taking their kid to the pediatrician, even if it's a major inconvenience. Most parents want to know the truth, good or bad, about their child's health. That's because parents love their kids and want to take care of them. So why would parents possibly object to state tests?

Well, think about the differences. Pediatricians give your child a checkup and then provide feedback in real time. Their task is to examine and treat *your* child. Check-ups are a brief, occasional inconvenience with a specific purpose. If there are problems, the physician will identify them, explain them, and suggest next steps or solutions.

Opt-out parents think that state testing is not *enough* like a doctor's visit. Test results aren't available until months after the test is taken, and sometimes not until the next school year. The tests are too broad to usefully inform classroom instruction. In fact, these tests are often justified not as a way to improve instruction but as a check on school and system performance. (For parents who trust their schools or distrust the tests, that's not a compelling rationale.) If a child does poorly, there's no guidance as to what the results mean or what to do about it. And it's not only the lengthy tests, but also the accompanying test prep and practice tests that parents may judge to be a pointless burden.

Do any of these concerns mean that opt-out parents are correct? Not at all. But opt-out parents are thinking like parents, and berating them for doing so seems unproductive and illogical. Reformers would be better served by listening to parental concerns, addressing them, and then using them to inform their designs.

Today, far too many schools, including "good" ones, are sedentary places of small-minded tedium. For lots of parents, contemporary efforts to promote accountability, turn around low-performing schools, or expand charter schooling haven't helped with any of this. If anything, these reforms seem to have hurt by making schools more stifling, narrow, and test-obsessed.

Parenthood has left me inclined to think that any parent who thinks reform is harming their kid deserves a respectful hearing. We can and should argue about whether they're right, but we should start by assuming that *all* parents are "for their kids."

19

Why History Matters

YEARS AGO, I PENNED A BOOK titled *The Same Thing Over and Over*. It was partly a history of American education, but it mostly tried to explain why school reform so often gets caught up in furious crusades that ultimately disappoint.[1]

I'd first seen how useful historical perspective could be back in 2001, when, as I mentioned several letters back, I wrote a controversial paper blasting teacher licensure.[2] I argued that licensure works best when there's agreement on essential skills and knowledge, but that those championing teacher licensure had trouble specifying precisely what those were.

Meanwhile, I argued, licensure was deterring many potentially promising teachers, doing little to ensure quality, and giving ed schools a gate-keeping role that fostered intellectual homogeneity. I proposed that, for the most part, states should adopt a model more like that used in business management or journalism—allowing anyone with a college degree to apply for a job, with employers taking it from there.

For our purposes, it doesn't matter what you think of the idea. I bring it up, though, because the whole episode taught me a lesson about the value of thinking historically about reform. The paper drew a fair bit of attention, including enthusiastic receptions from US Secretary of Education Rod Paige, the White House, and *USA Today* . . . and a lot of pretty hostile responses from my colleagues in education schools and teacher preparation. At the National Press Club, the head of the American Association of Colleges of Teacher Education suggested that my employer, the University of Virginia, ought to get rid of me.

This went on for months. At some point, as I spoke to various audiences, I hit upon the idea of explaining that licensure might have made sense when first adopted in the nineteenth century—as a way to ensure minimal teacher quality in a world where formal education and data were scarce—but that today it causes more problems than it solves.

This tack proved surprisingly productive. It reassured those who disagreed that I wasn't accusing them of nefarious motives. While most listeners still thought I was wrong, the history gave us a way to talk constructively about why certain policies were adopted, what had changed, and whether those policies still made sense. It also helped remind us that we were disagreeing more about means than about ends.

The experience left me convinced that a better understanding of why schools look the way they do can be a powerful tool for reform. I've found that talking about shifts in transportation, labor markets, and communication can provoke remarkably rewarding conversations about things like school governance and teacher pay.

Unfortunately, history doesn't show up too often when we're discussing school reform. Champions and critics of reform alike frequently ignore the fact that American schooling was never designed to do what we're asking of it today. Big-*R* Reformers approach their work with passion, an interest in research, and a desire to make change—but a limited understanding of how we got to the status quo. Meanwhile, critics routinely depict reforms as "attacks" on public education—as if our system of schooling were the product of a sacred design and not generations of compromise and happenstance. We have allowed these hand-me-down arrangements to shape our debates and define what counts as public education. For me, it's never been clear why yesterday's makeshift solutions to school governance, finance, or calendars should carry that kind of talismanic significance.

When I teach all of this, there's a brief quiz I use to help shake students out of some familiar assumptions. I ask questions like, "When were teacher step-and-lane pay scales first adopted?" "What share of American eighteen-year-olds were graduating high school in 1900?" "In the 1950s, what share of female college graduates went into teaching?" and "Across all of the nation's schools, combined, how many desktop computers were being used in 1960?"

Teacher step-and-lane pay was introduced in the early 1900s, but people have guessed anything from the 1700s to the 1980s. And while about one in ten Americans graduated from high school in 1900, a surprising number of people guess something closer to today's 80 percent. Over half of college-educated women became teachers in the 1950s, a time when other professions were largely closed to them. And in 1960, the nation's schools had no desktop computers . . . because they hadn't been invented yet. I've found this exercise helps to prompt reflection about what's changed over time, why it matters, and how rarely we think or talk about any of this.

After all, passion, research, and a desire for change might be enough to fuel reform if the schools erected over the past two centuries contained a blueprint for great teaching and learning in twenty-first-century America. But it's not clear that they do. Instead, I'd argue, they are rickety structures designed for different purposes and prone to wobbling under the weight of the new demands we've stacked on them.

In that spirit, let me give you the ninety-second version of what I spent two hundred pages discussing in *The Same Thing Over and Over*:

From the mid-1600s, when the Massachusetts Bay Colony adopted the first colonial educational policies, it took more than three centuries to build a school system that 90 percent of America's school-age youth attended daily. For the vast majority of that time, we asked schools to concentrate on molding students into God-fearing, authority-respecting citizens, without much concern for academic performance or "college readiness."

America's first great experiment in school reform was the "common school" push launched by Massachusetts school board chief Horace Mann in the 1830s and 1840s. Mann and his fellow reformers thought that packing kids into schools to read the King James Bible was the way to combat the menace of Catholic immigration. The common school strategy required a vast quantity of cheap, plentiful labor. The solution: turn teaching into women's work. Along the way, reformers feminized a teaching profession that had previously been mostly male.

As the twentieth century dawned, common schools were still expected to deliver only a rudimentary education to most children. At the time, just one in ten American eighteen-year-olds was graduating high school. A new generation of reformers thought much more was needed. They sought to universalize education by building a host of new schools, organizing them more systematically, and growing the teacher workforce. They relied heavily on importing "scientific management" methods used in private-sector factories. They championed top-down management, salary schedules, testing, and standardized record-keeping. Reformers trusted that smart, well-trained male administrators could improve schooling by using "best practices" to tightly control female teachers.

This kind of leadership yielded its share of capricious, dubious behavior. Teachers could be fired for getting married, being pregnant, or failing to conform to height and weight charts. Naturally enough, teachers responded by fighting for protections like tenure, work rules, and salary schedules. At the time, these wins were a sensible corrective to imperious management. They also meant, however, that teachers would be whipsawed between heavy-handed administrators on one side and increasingly rigid policies, meant to tame those administrators, on the other. The results, embedded in statute and contract, are still with us today.

The push to enroll more and more students—in order to get them off the streets, keep them out of the labor force, and socialize them properly—also made for diluted academic expectations. In 1918, for instance, the Commission on the Reorganization of Secondary Education famously held that schools needed to do far more to teach a growing student population how to make "worthy use of leisure."[3]

It was well into the twentieth century before we finally figured out how to get most of the nation's youth to school most of the time. Then, in short order, our goals radically changed. By the 1980s, warehousing and socialization were no longer the aim; we wanted schools to rigorously educate every child and ensure equal opportunity in a knowledge-based economy.

The goals were good and right. But they're also wildly ambitious. We're talking about fourteen thousand school systems and a hundred thousand schools that were primarily designed to teach basic skills, babysit, and combat moral turpitude. The architects of those schools and systems simply never had cause to ask, "Will these classrooms, budgeting rules, attendance requirements, or staffing practices help nurture powerful learning for all children in the twenty-first century?"

Today's reformers are engaged in a project that is far bigger and more ambitious than some may realize. Asking schools to make the shift we want is decidedly not a matter of "fixing" them. That's like thinking that you need to "fix" your kid's go-kart if it won't fly to Beijing. That doesn't make a lick of sense. Go-karts drive around the block; they don't fly to China. That's not a design flaw—they're just not built to do what you're asking. If you want a go-kart to *do* something entirely different, you may need to *design* something entirely different.

When reformers fail to recognize this, they can wind up spending an inordinate amount of energy fighting for policies that amount to putting new wheels on a rusty go-kart and hoping that will be enough for it to take flight. This would be okay if reformers expected these little changes to make a small difference. The problem is, they keep expecting this tinkering to make a *giant* difference.

I remember scratching my head a few years ago when the US Secretary of Education declared that the Common Core—an attempt to, at best, improve the quality of state reading and math standards—"may prove to be the single greatest thing to happen to public education in America since *Brown versus Board of Education*."[4] When modest changes don't yield big results, reformers get frustrated.

Things get even tougher because history teaches that many problems are not receptive to obvious "solutions." Take debates about how to balance standardized curricula and student-centered customization. We have bitter, ongoing fights over how to get this right. Guess what? We've been grappling with this tension since the dawn of Western civilization, when Plato entered the school reform wars and insisted on the need for standardized curricula and instruction. In *The Republic*, he called for the most scripted of curricula: "We must supervise the makers of tales . . . We'll persuade nurses and mothers to tell the approved tales to their children and to shape their souls with tales more than their bodies with hands."[5]

When Plato founded his famed Academy, however, he opted to customize the means, ends, and methods of schooling to suit each of his students.

How did the same guy who called for uber-standardized instruction justify this? He said that standardization was right for most but not all students—and that the students at the Academy were the kind who needed something different. In other words, he fudged it.

By ignoring centuries (or even millennia) of backstory, reformers are continually surprised by ineradicable tensions that aren't surprising at all. Thinking themselves the first to spy a challenge, they sprint off in search of a "fix." The result is a series of crusades that point first one way and then the other. High schools were once thought to be too small to offer a rich experience, then they were thought too big to be personal. Tracking was deemed essential to serve all students well, then denounced as a trap for students in the lower tracks. Vocational education was lauded for teaching useful skills, then dismissed as an academic backwater.

In each case, the concerns were reasonable. The attentive reformer will note, however, how incredibly hard it is to fine-tune these things or get them "right." Indeed, after enough time, we start to wonder whether we've overcorrected and then we reverse course once again. While those engaged in each successive charge are enthusiastic and sincere, the combined effect is to make reform an exhausting, circular march that stymies educators, sows confusion, and doesn't seem to get us anywhere.

At least for me, historical perspective suggests that reform is less a matter of "fixing" bad schools than of reinventing schools and systems. Personally, I'm disinclined to relitigate the decisions that got us here. What I do know is that those compromises weren't intended to ensure that all children would be rigorously educated or prepared for twenty-first-century citizenship. Knowing this can help reformers steer clear of straw men, scapegoats, and the temptation to vilify those who see things differently. And it can help emancipate them from outdated legacies.

Several years ago, the satirical site *The Onion* titled one of its faux news stories, "Historians Politely Remind Nation to Check What's Happened in Past Before Making Any Big Decisions."[6] It's funny, mostly because it's such good advice. The frustrating truth is that there are few permanent solutions for schools, only those that improve teaching and learning in a given place and at a given time. That's because reform is always a product of the available teaching force and technology, the needs of students, and the demands of the larger community.

This means two things for reformers. The first is that it's vital to question outmoded assumptions and routines if you're seeking more than cosmetic change. The second is that it's important to explain what's changed since the 1840s if you hope to convince parents, practitioners, and policymakers that your ideas are more than a mean-spirited attack on public education. In all of this, it turns out that history is an indispensable tool for the conscientious school reformer. Who'da thunk it?

20

Finding Your Way

I SOMETIMES GET ASKED for career advice by aspiring reformers. If you know me at all, you'll probably wonder about the wisdom in that. After all, as someone who works most of the year in shorts and flip-flops, I'm hardly a model of professional acumen. On the other hand, I *have* been doing this a long time and do have a few thoughts to share.

For starters, know that education is a funny business for those of us who don't work in schools. I remember the first time this really struck me. I'd just left teaching to go get my PhD. The first few weeks of the school year were tough. I was getting notes from former students. They weren't anything special, just funny stories and routine updates, but they were enough to make me really, really miss my classroom in Baton Rouge.

It's not like I was thinking, "Oh, man, they're lost without me." As a teacher, though, I'd felt like each day I was doing something real and important. Now I was reading soporific articles and engaging in esoteric debates.

A mentor gave me some good advice. A rotund, gruff guy, John Ameer had kept an eye on me since my days in Harvard's teacher preparation program. Tapped to help run that program after a long career as a principal, he'd been through this same transition. He said, "Rick, remember two things. The first is that life ebbs and flows. You were out there and now you're here. That's fine, so long as you did your best out there and you do your best now. You'll drive yourself nuts if you sit around thinking, 'Am I supposed to be there or here?'"

He paused. "Second, what we're doing here is a privilege. You've been in school for most of your life, so you take it for granted. But you shouldn't.

It's an amazing thing when reading is your job. When you've worked for a while, you'll understand. Just never imagine that what you're doing here is somehow more important than what you were doing in a classroom."

That helped. But when I'd thought about getting my doctorate, one big plus was having a "broader impact." I mentioned that. John's eyes twinkled as he said, "You think that way because you're still young. There are always trade-offs. You can have a profound impact on the lives of thirty students. Or you can change a law and, maybe, have a tiny, indirect impact on lots of students. I wouldn't be so quick to say one is 'broader.'"

Over time, I've met lots of young reformers struggling with their own questions. For better or worse, here are a few thoughts that some have found helpful.

A Job Isn't Forever. I've been impressed by how much twenty-somethings fret about which job is the right one. Guess what? When you take a job, you're not signing up forever. You're stepping into an opportunity to do some good, learn, grow, and meet people. If a job seems like it'll let you do those things, it's probably a terrific fit. Take it, enjoy it, work hard at it, and know you'll have a chance to reevaluate soon enough.

It's Cool to Do Different Things in Different Places. You'll learn different things from different jobs. If you're wondering which job will let you make an impact . . . well, it's a safe bet that they all will, in a variety of ways. It's good to work as a teacher or in schools; it's also good to work in communities and in states and in Washington. It's good to work for advocacy groups, reading programs, and for-profits; and for researchers and school districts and legislators. I'm *not* suggesting you should do all of this—just that all of it can be great and that you won't know what will feel most satisfying until you're there. A range of experiences will expose you to people with different skills, backgrounds, and views. All of that opens your eyes, informs your thinking, and helps you find your way.

There's Value in Working from the Inside and the Outside. Think of opportunities as arrayed along a continuum that spans from "inside" to "outside" the halls of power. Insiders get to be in the rooms where decisions are made and policies are crafted. They often work for elected officials or for foundations, associations, and advocacy groups that work closely with lawmakers. On the inside, you get to be part of a team working to get things done. But this comes at a price. You can't always speak your mind, especially in public. What you're getting done depends on what's politically practical. Outsiders are freer to speak their mind, surface radical solutions, and push new ideas. Of course, being on the outside also comes at a price. You aren't in the rooms where decisions are made. Insiders may hesitate to tell you things and will get frustrated with you. One isn't "better" or more important than another; they're just different. And relax—you can always move back and forth.

Watch Out for Thought Bubbles.   It's easy to talk only to people who think like you do. If you work for a group that's for charter schools or teacher leadership, you're probably going to work around people who share certain views. Colleagues will circulate articles and cite researchers who agree with those views, and may mock and dismiss those who lean the other way. Keep an eye out for thought bubbles and try to avoid stumbling into them.

Do Your Job.   When the New England Patriots won Super Bowl XLIX in 2015, they had a simple slogan: "Do your job." They won that game because a second-string cornerback named Malcolm Butler made a remarkable interception in the closing seconds. Butler studied hard, understood his role, and did the right thing at the right time. He did his job. There's a larger lesson here. It can feel like you're supposed to be "fixing" schools. If anyone knew how to "fix" education, though, they'd be racing around America doing it. The truth is that there are lots of jobs that need to be done and that are worth doing. There are programs to run, policies to shape, grants to give, arguments to make, facts to report, studies to conduct, critiques to offer, and much more. If you do your job and do it well, that's plenty. You won't be "fixing" education (no one else will be, either), but you'll be making a real contribution.

Take the Golden Rule Seriously. I must have been twenty-eight or twenty-nine, and it was one of the first times I was on a panel at a major conference. The topic was teacher recruitment and training. A fellow panelist was saying things that struck me as foolish. As he spoke, I could have taken notes, made a grocery list, or daydreamed about the beach. Instead, I rolled my eyes. I sighed. I went out of the way to show how uninterested I was. It was an arrogant, cringeworthy display. Fortunately, a thoughtful colleague took me aside, put a hand on my shoulder, and gave it to me straight. She told me that my display was unprofessional and self-defeating. She said, "Rick, you might've been saying important things, but I wouldn't know because I was so distracted by you behaving like an ass. If you want respect, you have to give respect." It was a lesson I've never forgotten.

Embrace the 90-10 Rule. On their first day, I usually talk to my new hires about the "90-10" rule. It's simple. Ninety percent of any job is within your control, and 10 percent is out of your hands. I expect my staff to own the 90 percent: be prompt, detail-oriented, smart, and organized. Even when they do that, though, stuff will go wrong, and I expect them to think on their feet to solve that other 10 percent as best they can. Flights get canceled. Bomb threats get phoned in. Capuchin monkeys escape from the workshop down the hall and leap onstage. Their job isn't to ensure that the world works perfectly, but to nail the 90 percent—and show their mettle by handling the 10 percent when things get goofy. The same goes for you.

Make Deposits in the Favor Bank. If you've never read Tom Wolfe's *The Bonfire of the Vanities*, you should. In Wolfe's masterpiece, flamboyant lawyer Tommy Killian explains the favor bank: "Everything in this building, everything in the criminal justice system in New York . . . operates on favors. Everybody does favors for everybody else."[1] I've found that education operates the same way. When you can, help people out. Solve a problem, put in a good word, make someone's life easier. Especially when you're young and in a hurry, doing favors can seem like a needless distraction. It's not. People appreciate these things, they remember them, and they repay them in kind.

Presume Good Intentions. Because they mean well, think they're smart, and spend a lot of time with like-minded friends, reformers can wind up being self-righteous and dismissive of those who disagree. Keep in mind that almost everyone in and around education means well. If you doubt other people's motives, work to put yourself in their shoes, master their arguments, and get to know them. Nine times out of ten, I've found, you can respect where they're coming from and learn from it—even if you still vehemently disagree.

Don't Get Too Impressed with Yourself. Reformers can find themselves sitting on panels, testifying to legislatures, writing op-eds, advising elected officials, and appearing on radio or TV. Young reformers can get written up in profiles of "30 leaders under 30." All of this can lead to an inflated sense of yourself and your expertise. That can offend colleagues and will assuredly alienate educators, who are too busy teaching to do that stuff. Keeping your head level can be especially tough when you don't have a lot of experience. But the world has a way of humbling you. Years ago, I remember heading up to Toronto to deliver one of my first big talks. I had a featured spot in the program. The venue probably held a thousand people. I was feeling good. Then about three dozen people showed up. That's a *lot* of empty seats. Keep yourself grounded, so the world doesn't have to do it for you.

Sweat the Small Stuff. Little things make a big difference. Most reformers I've known are mission-driven and animated by grand ideas. That's great. The downside is that it leaves some disinclined to sweat mundane things like planning, deadlines, or details. Set yourself apart by being responsive and reliable. Even in the most casual of environs, it'll help you make a difference, your colleagues will appreciate it, and others will notice it.

Unleash Your Brain. If you're smart and humble, it can seem like sweating the small stuff means doing exactly what you're told. Period. That's a mistake. People need colleagues who figure things out and help solve problems. Be a solution finder and not just a direction taker. One of the big advantages of youth is that you've had less time to settle into familiar routines and relationships. Make that work for you. Find opportunities to read, ruminate, and explore. Seek out provocative research, connect with new people, and surface unconventional ideas. Look for opportunities to plan, write, or take responsibility for a project or program. Sweat the small stuff, but do it with an energetic, inquisitive mind.

Keep Your Word. Too many reformers promise to do something and then get distracted, overwhelmed, or just forget. That's a deal-breaker. It means other people can't rely on you or give you meaningful responsibility. Do what you say you'll do, and do it when you say you will.

If you work hard, take care to be civil and reliable, and make it a point to unleash your brain, opportunities will find you. Because here's a dirty little secret: it's much harder to find talent than you might expect. Everybody, everywhere is always seeking competent, passionate problem solvers. If you strive to be one, you'll be fine.

I like my job but never had a clue I'd be doing it—until the day I was hired. At the time, I was a professor and liked being one. The problem was that I kept getting in hot water. I wanted to be somewhere where I could be myself without creating headaches, but I had no clue how to find that place. So I did my job. I worked hard, got to know people, and got inquiries, including from the president of the American Enterprise Institute (AEI)—a place I barely knew. It turned out that AEI had been trying to launch an education policy program for years. A couple of mentors had suggested my name to him. He and I talked, then talked some more, and here I am.

That's the point. Education is a sprawling field with lots of opportunities to make a difference. Don't spend too much time worrying about which role is the right one. Find roles that are interesting, where you'll do something worthwhile, and where you'll work with good people who can teach you things. Learn, both from those with whom you agree and from those with whom you don't. If you do that, things have a funny way of working out.

21

The Perils of Passion

IN 2014, DAVID FRENCH, an Iraq War veteran, Bronze Star recipient, constitutional lawyer, author, and all-around fascinating guy, delivered a commencement speech that school reformers should take to heart. It's worth quoting at length here because French so elegantly captures how passion can lead us astray. He told the graduates:

> When I was your age, I knew a lot more than I know now. I was a voracious reader—my parents still have pictures of me sitting on the floor with encyclopedias fanned out around me—and my reading taught me what I needed to know. And oh, how I lorded that knowledge over my less well-read peers.
>
> In hindsight, I must have been moderately insufferable.
>
> I thought I knew about the homeless, until I spent night after night in shelters in Nashville, talking to them, sleeping next to them, and making meals.
>
> I thought I knew about inner cities, until I mentored a kid from the projects in East Nashville and gained just the smallest insights into his world.
>
> I thought I knew how to help the poor, until my wife and I reached out to the poorest and most desperate members of our community, naively certain that our love, concern, and money was enough—enough to change lives.
>
> And I thought I knew about war, until I went to fight, lost friends, and saw the reality with my own eyes.
>
> By God's grace, I pray I'll never think I know as much as I once thought I did.[1]

I wish I could say it half as well. Don't get me wrong: there is still much that I think I know. For instance, I think that those making decisions should be responsible for making them work; that schools and educators should be accountable for whether kids are learning; that people who are good at their jobs should get more money and recognition than those who aren't; and that bureaucratic routine is a lousy way to cultivate great schools. And I think that policy can make people do things, but can't make them do them well—and that, when it comes to school reform, what usually matters is how, rather than whether, things are done.

As far as knowing the "right" way to do any of this, though? There, I'm afraid that I know less now than I did when I got started in school reform twenty-five years ago. It's always possible that you're much smarter, wiser, and more knowledgeable than I am, so perhaps my qualms shouldn't apply to you.

But I'm betting they should, given how many years I've spent watching reformers operate with more surety than success.

I recall lunch with a state education official in Denver. This must have been around 2012, when the Common Core was first encountering headwinds. We didn't really know each other, but we were in town for the same gathering. He had seen me give a talk on educational entrepreneurship and reached out. He wanted to learn more. He was a pleasant, thoughtful guy with his share of amusing stories. We were having a genial conversation until we got into the Common Core. He was passionate about the Common Core and clearly assumed that anyone who'd really thought it through would be equally enthusiastic. I wasn't.

The issue was obviously personal for him. He couldn't let it drop. He kept asking about my reservations and then dismissing them. His mouth grew tight. His face gradually reddened. He took to slapping the table for emphasis. He clearly thought I'd been duped, didn't get it, or didn't really care about kids. His passion had closed the door to a fruitful discussion. I sat there wondering what had happened to the thoughtful guy I'd been talking to twenty minutes earlier.

Passion is an amazing thing. It's what enables us to get big stuff done. Harvard football coach Tim Murphy, owner of eight Ivy League titles, puts it well: "There's only one way you can do this job: 100 miles an hour and your hair on fire."[2]

In schooling, the best practitioners and reformers alike are passionate about their work. Their commitment can be heart-warming, inspiring, even intimidating.

But passion's very intensity can distort our vision. Most Americans, for example, will tell pollsters that a fair political compromise is one in which Republicans and Democrats each get half of what they want. But passionate partisans see things differently. Voters who are intensely liberal think Democrats should get two-thirds of what they want in any deal, while their counterparts on the right say the same about Republicans. Compromise looks different to the impassioned than it does to others.[3]

Passion can stymie careful analysis and stifle good judgment. Ryan Holiday, bestselling author and editor-at-large at *Betabeat*, puts it elegantly in a 2014 essay examining the "passion paradox":

> Passion may be the very thing holding you back from success . . . Problems are not solved with an uncontrollable flash of genius or creativity, but with sober reflection, strategy and execution. We don't go in fueled by adrenaline, guns blazing. Rather, a solution is a well-aimed bullet fired with a steady hand. And passion is not the slug. It's the gunpowder. Remember in *Jerry Maguire*, how he has an epiphany and stays up all night in a passion-fueled frenzy writing his manifesto? What happens? He goes in the next day and gets f***ing fired.

Holiday continues with a riff that every reformer should take to heart:

> Deliberateness and passion are almost always at odds with each other the more critical the situation becomes. My dog is passionate. She is not deliberate and her purpose is fleeting from one moment to the next. As numerous squirrels, birds, boxes, blankets and toys can tell you—she does not accomplish most of what she sets out to do . . . Passion makes people delusional. Because passion is ego and selfishness. It is narrative. It's saying with a straight face: "I'm going to do [insert preposterous things that never happen]" . . . How can [people] say these things and believe them? Because passion blinds us, it mutes our empathy and tells us what we want to hear about ourselves . . . It feels like you're going in the right direction, when in reality you're not going anywhere at all. That's what I want you to understand. Passion isn't helping. Not if you're trying to do big things. We don't

need you to be excited or jazzed. The world has that in spades. It'd actually be far better if you were intimidated by what lay ahead—humbled by its magnitude and determined to see it through regardless.[4]

This could have been written just for school reformers. Indeed, reformers display some disconcerting similarities to Holiday's impassioned dog, chasing after every squirrel that comes along and thus catching hardly any of them. Reformers get fired up about an issue, insist that the status quo is intolerable, bang the drum about their newfound cause for a couple years . . . and then move on to new concerns. Impassioned advocates can find it more exhilarating and rewarding to tackle the next pioneering policy change than to grind away on last year's big idea. This is all natural, and none of it is ill intentioned. But the result is often bad for schooling and bad for kids.

Passion also creates a "do something" bias that can get reformers in trouble. Confronted with a problem, passion fuels the admirable urge to do *something*. Educators have lots of ways to channel this impulse into concrete actions that aid students. They can provide extra tutoring, revamp lesson plans, or reach out to parents. Reformers generally don't have similarly satisfying options at their disposal. When reformers insist on doing "something," it usually means calling for big changes to what other people do. So they propose flurries of initiatives and policies. Since there are lots of problems to address and since passion makes each seem urgent, this can contribute to mad swings from one enthusiasm to the next. This passion-fueled churning means reforms frequently disappear or else get adopted hastily and with little follow-through.

Things get worse when hair-on-fire passion causes good reformers to burn out. Long hours worked at maximum intensity will exhaust anyone. Passion can lead reformers to take victories and setbacks too personally, and that's emotionally draining. Burnout leads to an inopportune loss of memory and experience, especially when it means that reformers who were pivotal in major policy victories may not be around for the aftermath.

And, truth be told, passion can make us dumb. When I was still at the University of Virginia, I did a fair bit of work for the Houston-based Center for Reform of School Systems (CRSS). I recall a time we were huddling over doughnuts with a school board member from one of Ohio's big cities. She was hoping to organize a citywide school reform summit. Don McAdams, the founder of CRSS, had served three terms on the Houston school board. He listened and offered some measured thoughts. Me? I loved the idea. I was fired up. I leapt up and started pacing, waving my hands, offering up suggestions at a mile a minute. Don looked like he couldn't decide whether to laugh or sigh. The woman looked shell-shocked. I may have single-handedly killed the idea. I'd like to blame the doughnuts, but I can't. It was just old-fashioned, undirected passion trouncing my common sense.

The urgency and optimism borne of passion can tempt us to wave away complexity. That's been a problem for generations of reformers. I've always found the old parable about "stone soup" instructive in explaining why. In case you don't remember it: After the Revolutionary War, three soldiers were making their way home through the New England winter. Cold and hungry, they came upon a village. They knocked on doors, asking for carrots, onions, rabbit—anything that villagers could spare—only to get turned away. Finally, the soldiers knocked on a door and asked only for a cooking pot. The villager said, "Sure." The soldiers filled the pot with water from a nearby stream, built a fire in the middle of the village, and set the pot on to boil.

When a couple of villagers stopped by to see what was up, one of the soldiers tossed a large stone into the pot. When a villager asked about the stone, the soldier explained, "We're making stone soup. When it's ready, you can have some. It's amazing. You'll love it." He paused. "The only thing," he said, "is that it's even better with a little carrot." The villager said, "I've got some carrots. I'll go grab a couple." After those got tossed in, the soldier mused, "This is going to be sensational, but stone soup is better still with a little onion." Another villager popped home and brought back a few onions. By the end, the pot was filled with good stuff, the soldiers gorged themselves, and the villagers all agreed that stone soup was the best soup they'd ever had.

The tale should feel familiar to anyone who has seen promising school reforms dazzle and then disappoint. Pilot programs invariably benefit from enthusiastic leadership, foundation support, intense hand-holding from experts, waivers from contracts and district regulations, energized teachers and families, and more. Not surprisingly, things tend to work pretty well. Wooed by promising results, imitators try to scale the innovation to new sites that lack these advantages. The result? The reform disappoints and onlookers lament the implementation problems. The "reform" amounts to the stone in the soup. When other schools or systems try it, the other ingredients usually get left out and would-be imitators wind up sipping hot pebble-water.

In the grip of passion, it's all too easy to overlook these pitfalls. Even after scores of similar failures, an ardent reformer can insist, "But this stone works so damn well! I'm sure we'll see these same results elsewhere, even without those other frills." Thus, school reform starts to resemble Charlie Brown's perpetual race to kick that football, only to be thwarted each time Lucy yanks it away. Passion leads reformers to redouble their efforts, seeking an even *better* stone or a way to run to the ball even *faster*. Perhaps not so surprisingly, this doesn't usually work.

In the end, the measure of reformers' seriousness isn't simply their passion but whether they yoke that passion to forethought, humility, and reflection. This means not just citing evidence that you like and dismissing the rest. It means knowing that reform involves winners and losers, values and unanticipated consequences, and is almost never a simple question of "what works."

If we're being honest with one another, we're inevitably going to disagree about a lot of this. Serious school reformers see disagreement as okay—as a blessing borne of our liberty, democracy, and diversity—and not as *prima facie* evidence of another's lack of passion.

I'll leave you with this: It's good to be passionate about education. It's right that you be relentless in fighting for the reforms you believe in. But, when all is said and done, you need to pursue your passion with a professional discipline to match. I don't have much use for a surgeon who's so impassioned that she can't see straight or a marine sergeant so gung-ho that he needlessly exposes his unit to danger. In every field, the professional is responsible for marrying passion and professionalism. That holds for school reformers as well.

It can be a helluva challenge to embrace that discipline when your passion boils over. I get it. I've certainly fallen short time and again. But that's my compass. I hope you choose to make it yours.

A Few Final Thoughts

I'VE SAID MY PIECE. I don't want to draw this out unnecessarily. But, given that we've come this far together, a few final thoughts seem in order.

As I promised at the start, I've tried to focus on the *how* rather than the *what* of reform. This is because I've come to believe that reform can either hurt or help, and the answer depends greatly on how reforms are designed and pursued. Whatever your vision for change, I hope these letters help you pursue it in a manner more likely to mean good things for students and educators. If you're inclined to raise an eyebrow at that mention of educators and insist, "This is about kids, not adults!" . . . well, I think you're wrong. After all, policy is good at making people do things, and that can be enough if the goal is to ensure that schools report daily attendance or provide a hot lunch to students. When the *how* matters most, though, what educators think is crucial. For better or worse, good schools are the product of thousands of tiny judgments that those educators make every day. Sure, some educators are inept and others resist change, but reform is ultimately about creating schools where educators can do their best work. When reformers can't get lots of educators—especially accomplished ones—on board, introspection is in order.

Some of what I've had to say regarding the limitations of research, data, and expertise may strike impassioned reformers as negative or even nihilistic. They may regard the constraints and cautions I've raised as a disheartening litany. That's not how I see it. Research, data, and expertise have a great deal to offer. The problem is *not* with these powerful tools, but with the cavalier, unskilled, and even disingenuous way they've sometimes been used. I'm all for assessments designed by experts, reading instruction informed by rigorous research, and hiring decisions informed by careful metrics. What I can't endorse, and what can be harmful, is when reformers use these things to promote half-baked agendas, silence skeptics, and avoid inconvenient questions.

Reform has had signal successes over the past two decades: more transparency, higher expectations, more room for creative problem-solving, more options for families, terrific models of tech-inspired redesign, and much more. While none of this has "fixed" schools, it has done good things for a lot of kids. Because young reformers keep hearing that their job is to "take it to scale," however, these modest successes can feel distinctly unsatisfying. If you're feverishly seeking to make schools better everywhere, in a hurry, anything less can seem like surrender. It shouldn't. It's tough to scale complex processes or skills. If you want to scale a learning management system or software for tracking school expenditures, have at it. If you want to grow a promising charter model from five schools to fifty, that's harder but manageable. If, though, you're hoping to sit in a state capital and develop the policies or programs that will rapidly "fix" hundreds or thousands of schools, disappointment awaits. This isn't downbeat or pessimistic; it's just how things are. The search for scale is healthy, but shortcuts won't get you there.

Speaking of which, neither will YouTube videos. In recent years, big-*R* Reform has sometimes felt like it's headquartered in a political campaign's war room. I've been struck by the growing fascination with PR campaigns and political strategies. There's a place for both substance and messaging, of course, but I've seen attention to political tactics come at the expense of deliberation and honest self-appraisal. Eager to draw attention and show funders an "impact," reformers have found it ever easier to get caught up in the thrill of the hunt. This makes me think that it's a good time to be more deliberate. To speak and write more selectively. To be more discerning about the gatherings we host and attend. We're swimming in noise. There's a yawning need for reflection and a willingness to listen to one another. It's tough to listen, though, if we're constantly chattering, and it's even tougher if we're shouting.

Since we're nearing the end, I'll offer a confession: I'm not an especially nice guy. When I suggest that reformers should listen to those who disagree, that reformers are well-served by humility, or that reform needs to work for teachers as well as for students, it's not because I want everyone to get along. It's because education reform is hard. Doing it well is at least at much about discipline and precision as it is about passion. What I'm counseling is not niceness but *professionalism*. At times, some readers may feel like I'm picking on reformers. I don't think that's quite right. After all, I've spent years telling educators they have a responsibility to help reinvent schools; they can't just kvetch and complain about reform. Reformers have reciprocal obligations. What I've tried to offer is a corrective to heedless passion and well-meaning miscalculation. I want to help reformers discipline and harness their passion. A decade ago, I penned a book titled *Tough Love for Schools*. You won't be far off the mark if you think of this volume as *Tough Love for School Reform*.

If there's one lesson I hope I've impressed on you, it's the importance of talking *to* people rather than *at* them. It's easy (especially when you're young and impassioned) to see issues in black and white and be confident you know the right answers. Solving other people's problems, however, requires understanding their concerns. That means talking to those with whom you disagree. Otherwise, you'll find yourself asking why those knuckleheads are so unappreciative, why they're resisting your good ideas, and why things aren't working out as intended. If it helps, know that I keep finding that people I was inclined to dismiss are nicer, more thoughtful, and better intentioned than I'd assumed. Forging friendships with those who disagree is especially helpful because, while a stranger may teach us something, it's our friends who can really help us see things in a new light.

One last thing. For 99 percent of families out there, school reform isn't about research, the future workforce, or the pursuit of "social justice." It's about their children, right here, right now. Period. I've never loved anyone like I love my boys. It pains me when my kids get frustrated or bang a knee, and it cheers me when they do something the least bit clever or kind. As a parent, all I want from schools is that they give my boys every chance to live good lives and be good citizens. That's all any parent wants. School reformers have the marvelous, inspiring mission of helping to make that happen. But, as reformers, we're strangers to almost all the students and families out there. What's an impassioned cause for reformers is personal and visceral for parents. Whatever you think of them, it's *always* a mistake to dismiss their concerns as ill informed, misguided, or selfish. Far too many bungled reforms have come and gone for you to expect anyone to accept your agenda on faith. Take responsibility for giving them reason to trust. You know, it may have been Spider-Man's Uncle Ben who said it best when he cautioned young Peter Parker, "With great power comes great responsibility." If you're hoping to be a school reform superhero, those are pretty good words to live by.

Notes

Preface

1. Francisco Castillo, "MEMO: A Big Night for Education Reform: Three Elections, Three Wins for Pro-Reform Candidates," StudentsFirst, June 6, 2012, https://www.studentsfirst.org/blogs /entry/memo-a-big-night-for-education-reform-three-elections-three-wins-for-pro-re.
2. Joel Ben Izzy, *The Beggar King and the Secret of Happiness* (Chapel Hill, NC: Algonquin Books, 2003).

Chapter 1

1. Nikhil Goyal, *One Size Does Not Fit All: A Student's Assessment of School* (Roslyn Heights, NY: Alternative Education Resource Organization, 2012).
2. Frederick M. Hess, *Spinning Wheels: The Politics of Urban School Reform* (Washington, DC: Brookings Institution Press, 1998), 95.

Chapter 2

1. Theodore Roosevelt, "The Man in the Arena," excerpt from "Citizenship in a Republic," http://www.theodore-roosevelt.com/trsorbonnespeech.html.
2. Frederick M. Hess, "Oregon School Boards Assoc.: Wuv Us, Dammit!" *Education Week*, February 8, 2012, http://blogs.edweek.org/edweek/rick_hess_straight_up/2012/02/oregon _school_boards_assoc_wuv_us_dammit.html.

Chapter 3

1. Pew Research Center, "Section 3: Political Polarization and Personal Life," *Political Polarization in the American Public*, June 12, 2014, http://www.people-press.org/2014/06/12 /section-3-political-polarization-and-personal-life/.
2. John Buccigross, "Time to Give the West Its Due," ESPN, February 2, 2010, http://espn.go .com/nhl/notebook/_/page/buccigross_100202/nhl-east-coast-bias-john-buccigross-looks -balance-nhl-scales.
3. Scott Page, *The Difference: How the Power of Diversity Creates Better Groups, Firms, Schools, and Societies* (Princeton, NJ: Princeton University Press, 2008), 137.
4. Ibid., 138.

5. Samuel R. Sommers, "On Racial Diversity and Group Decision Making: Identifying Multiple Effects of Racial Composition on Jury Deliberations," *Journal of Personality and Social Psychology* 90 (2006), doi:10.1037/0022-3514.90.4.597.

6. Irving L. Janis, "Groupthink," *Psychology Today* (1971), http://agcommtheory.pbworks.com /f/GroupThink.pdf.

7. Kathrin Lassila, "A Brief History of Groupthink: Why Two, Three, or Many Heads Aren't Always Better Than One," *Yale Alumni Magazine*, January/February 2008, https://yalealumni magazine.com/articles/1947/a-brief-history-of-groupthink.

Chapter 4

1. Daniel Weisberg, Susan Sexton, Jennifer Mulhern, and David Keeling, *The Widget Effect: Our National Failure to Acknowledge and Act on Differences in Teacher Effectiveness*, 2nd ed., The New Teacher Project, 2009, http://tntp.org/assets/documents/TheWidgetEffect_2nd_ed.pdf.

2. Michael B. Henderson, Paul E. Peterson, and Martin R. West, "No Common Opinion on the Common Core," *Education Next* 15, no. 1 (2015), http://educationnext.org/2014-ednext-poll -no-common-opinion-on-the-common-core/.

3. "Governor Scott Signs Student Success Act," flgov.com, March 24, 2011, http://www.flgov .com/2011/03/24/governor-scott-signs-student-success-act/; Rick Outzen, "Scott Signs Bill Tying Teacher Pay to Test Scores, Ends Tenure," *Rick's Blog*, March 24, 2011, http://ricksblog .biz/scott-signs-bill-tying-teacher-pay-to-test-scores-ends-tenure/comment-page-1/.

4. Matthew A. Kraft and Allison F. Gilmour, "Revisiting *The Widget Effect*: Teacher Evaluation Reforms and the Distribution of Teacher Effectiveness," July 2016, http://scholar.harvard.edu /mkraft/publications/revisiting-widget-effect-teacher-evaluation-reforms-and-distribution -teacher.

5. Frederick M. Hess, *The Cage-Busting Teacher* (Cambridge, MA: Harvard Education Press, 2015), 91.

6. Ibid., 93.

7. Frederick M. Hess, "Tear Down This Wall: The Case for a Radical Overhaul of Teacher Certification," *Educational Horizons* 80, no. 4 (2002), https://www.jstor.org/stable/42927125 ?seq=1#page_scan_tab_contents.

Chapter 5

1. Emily Shire, "The Amazing Tale of Paul the Psychic Octopus: Germany's World Cup Soothsayer," *The Daily Beast*, July 12, 2014, http://www.thedailybeast.com/articles/2014/07/12 /remembering-paul-the-psychic-octopus-germany-s-2010-world-cup-soothsayer.html.

2. Maxime Rieman, "Study: Only 24% of Active Mutual Fund Managers Outperform the Market Index," *NerdWallet*, March 27, 2013, https://www.nerdwallet.com/blog/investing /investing-data/active-mutual-fund-managers-beat-market-index/; Tyler Durden, "Wall Street Is a Rentier Rip-Off: Index Funds Beat 99.6% of Managers over Ten Years," *Zero Hedge*, April 29, 2013, http://www.zerohedge.com/news/2013-04-29/wall-street-rentier-rip-index -funds-beat-996-managers-over-ten-years.

3. Noreena Hertz, "How to Use Experts—and When Not To," TED, February 2011, https://www .ted.com/talks/noreena_hertz_how_to_use_experts_and_when_not_to/transcript.

4. Jason Zweig, "This Is Your Brain on Investment Advice," *Wall Street Journal*, March 31, 2009, http://blogs.wsj.com/wallet/2009/03/31/this-is-your-brain-on-investment-advice/.

5. Ewen Callaway, "Brain Quirk Could Help Explain Financial Crisis," *New Scientist*, March 24, 2009, https://www.newscientist.com/article/dn16826-brain-quirk-could-help-explain -financial-crisis/.

6. "Best-Sellers Initially Rejected," *LitRejections*, http://www.litrejections.com/best-sellers -initially-rejected/.

7. Louis Menand, "Everybody's an Expert," *The New Yorker*, December 5, 2005, http://www .newyorker.com/magazine/2005/12/05/everybodys-an-expert.

8. Herbert Hoover, "Inaugural Address of Herbert Hoover: March 24, 1929," Herbert Hoover Presidential Library and Museum, http://www.hoover.archives.gov/info/inauguralspeech .html.

9. Kevin Fogarty, "Tech Predictions Gone Wrong," *ComputerWorld*, October 22, 2012, http:// www.computerworld.com/article/2492617/it-management/tech-predictions-gone-wrong .html.

10. "Things People Said: Bad Predictions," RinkWorks, http://www.rinkworks.com/said /predictions.shtml.

Chapter 7

1. Office of the Press Secretary, "Remarks by the President on 'My Brother's Keeper' Initiative," The White House, February 27, 2014, https://www.whitehouse.gov/the-press-office/2014/02 /27/remarks-president-my-brothers-keeper-initiative.

Chapter 8

1. "Examples of Campbell's Law," May 24, 2013, http://www.xamuel.com/examples-of -campbells-law/.

2. Laurence Zuckerman, "In Airline Math, an Early Arrival Doesn't Mean You Won't Be Late," *New York Times*, December 26, 2000, http://www.nytimes.com/2000/12/26/business/in -airline-math-an-early-arrival-doesn-t-mean-you-won-t-be-late.html.

3. Paul Craig Roberts and Katharine LaFollette, *Meltdown: Inside the Soviet Economy* (Washington, DC: Cato Institute, 1990).

4. "Examples of Campbell's Law"; Tony Waters, "Campbell's Law, Planned Social Change, Vietnam War Deaths, and Condom Distributions in Refugee Camps," Ethnography.com, April 22, 2015, http://www.ethnography.com/2015/04/campbells-law-planned-social -change-vietnam-war-deaths-and-condom-distributions-in-refugee-camps/.

5. Michael Lewis, *Moneyball: The Art of Winning an Unfair Game* (New York: W.W. Norton & Company, 2004).

Chapter 9

1. Stuart Jeffries, "House of Cards Recap: Season Two, Episode Three: 'Doormats and Matadors,'" *The Guardian*, February 21, 2014, http://www.theguardian.com/tv-and-radio/tv andradioblog/2014/feb/21/house-of-cards-season-two-episode-three.

2. Frederick M. Hess, *Spinning Wheels: The Politics of Urban School Reform* (Washington, DC: Brookings Institution Press, 1998), 95.

3. Allan R. Cohen and David L. Bradford, *Influence Without Authority*, 2nd ed. (Hoboken, NJ: Wiley, 2005).

4. Mike Feinberg, "Cage-Busting in the Early Years," *Education Week*, March 1, 2013, http://blogs .edweek.org/edweek/rick_hess_straight_up/2013/03/cage-busting_in_the_early_years.html.

Chapter 10

1. Benedict Carey, "Many Psychology Findings Not as Strong as Claimed, Study Says," *New York Times*, August 27, 2015, http://www.nytimes.com/2015/08/28/science/many-social -science-findings-not-as-strong-as-claimed-study-says.html.

2. Leslie K. John, George Loewenstein, and Drazen Prelec, "Measuring the Prevalence of Questionable Research Practices with Incentives for Truth Telling," *Association for Psychological Science*, 2012, http://www.cmu.edu/dietrich/sds/docs/loewenstein/MeasPrevalQuestTruth Telling.pdf.

3. Diane Whitmore Schanzenbach, "Does Class Size Matter?" National Education Policy Center, February 18, 2014, http://nepc.colorado.edu/publication/does-class-size-matter.

4. James J. Heckman, "Letters to the Editor: Early Childhood Education Can Yield Economic Rewards," *Washington Post*, July 19, 2013, https://www.washingtonpost.com/opinions/early -childhood-education-can-yield-economic-rewards/2013/07/19/35a302a8-efcb-11e2-8c36 -0e868255a989_story.html.

5. See, for example, Stephen Sawchuk, "Merit Pay Found to Have Little Effect on Achievement," *Education Week*, September 21, 2010, http://www.edweek.org/ew/articles/2010/09/21/05pay _ep.h30.html.

Chapter 11

1. Frederick M. Hess, "Is Anybody Up for Defending the Common Core Math Standards?" *Education Next*, September 6, 2011, http://educationnext.org/is-anybody-up-for-defending -the-common-core-math-standards/.

2. Lyndsey Layton, "How Bill Gates Pulled Off the Swift Common Core Revolution," *Washington Post*, June 7, 2014, https://www.washingtonpost.com/politics/how-bill-gates-pulled-off -the-swift-common-core-revolution/2014/06/07/a830e32e-ec34-11e3-9f5c-9075d5508f0a _story.html.

3. Press Office, "Duncan Pushes Back on Attacks on Common Core Standards," US Department of Education, June 25, 2013, http://www.ed.gov/news/speeches/duncan-pushes-back-attacks -common-core-standards; Valerie Strauss, "Arne Duncan: 'White Suburban Moms' Upset That Common Core Shows Their Kids Aren't 'Brilliant,'" *Washington Post*, November 16, 2013, https://www.washingtonpost.com/news/answer-sheet/wp/2013/11/16/arne-duncan -white-surburban-moms-upset-that-common-core-shows-their-kids-arent-brilliant/.

Chapter 12

1. John Fensterwald, "California Appeals Court Overturns Vergara Ruling," *EdSource*, April 14, 2016, https://edsource.org/2016/california-appeals-court-overturns-vergara-ruling/562855.

2. Rolf M. Treu, *Vergara v. State of California*, 2014, https://www.documentcloud.org/documents /1184998-vergara-tentativedecision061014.html.

3. Joshua M. Dunn, "Courting Education: Mitigating the Seven (Somewhat) Deadly Sins of Education Litigation," in *Carrots, Sticks, and the Bully Pulpit: Lessons from a Half-Century of Federal Efforts to Improve America's Schools*, ed. Frederick M. Hess and Andrew P. Kelly (Cambridge, MA: Harvard Education Press, 2012), 83–84.

4. Charles Dickens, *Bleak House*, vol. 1, chapter 3, 1853, https://books.google.com/books?id =KlsJAAAAQAAJ.

5. Valerie Strauss, "A Silver Lining in the Vergara Decision?" *Washington Post*, June 11, 2014, https://www.washingtonpost.com/news/answer-sheet/wp/2014/06/11/a-silver-lining-in-the -vergara-decision/.

Chapter 13

1. Mark Goodburn, "What Is The Life Expectancy of Your Company?" World Economic Forum, January 24, 2015, https://www.weforum.org/agenda/2015/01/what-is-the-life-expectancy-of -your-company/.

2. Morgan Brown, "Airbnb: The Growth Story You Didn't Know," Growth Hackers, n.d., https://growthhackers.com/growth-studies/airbnb.

3. For more extensive profiles of both schools, see Frederick M. Hess and Bror Saxberg, *Breakthrough Leadership in the Digital Age: Using Learning Science to Reboot Schooling* (Thousand Oaks, CA: Corwin Press, 2014).

4. Thomas Stewart and Patrick J. Wolf, "The School Choice Journey: Parents Experiencing More Than Improved Test Scores," American Enterprise Institute, January 26, 2015, https://www.aei.org/publication/school-choice-journey-parents-experiencing-improved-test-scores/.

Chapter 14

1. Larry Cuban, *Oversold and Underused: Computers in the Classroom* (Cambridge, MA: Harvard University Press, 2003).

2. Catherine Clifford, "5 Entrepreneurial Lessons from Uber on Its 5-Year Anniversary," *Entrepreneur,* June 4, 2015, https://www.entrepreneur.com/article/247014.

3. Bettina Fabos, *Wrong Turn on the Information Superhighway: Education and the Commercialization of the Internet* (New York: Teachers College Press, 2004), 1, http://www.uni.edu/fabos/publications/wrongturnch.1-history.pdf.

4. Larry Cuban, *Teachers and Machines: The Classroom Use of Technology Since 1920* (New York: Teachers College Press, 1986), 19.

5. Frederick M. Hess and Bror Saxberg, *Breakthrough Leadership in the Digital Age: Using Learning Science to Reboot Schooling* (Thousand Oaks, CA: Corwin Press, 2014).

6. Nate Silver, *The Signal and the Noise: Why So Many Predictions Fail—but Some Don't* (New York: Penguin Books, 2012), 2–3.

7. Johannes Trithemius, *In Praise of Scribes*, trans. Robert Behrendt, ed. Klaus Arnold (Lawrence, KS: Coronado Press, 1974).

Chapter 15

1. Frederick M. Hess, "A Mantra for K–12 Philanthropy: First, Do No Harm," *Education Week,* July 16, 2014, http://www.edweek.org/ew/articles/2014/07/16/37hess.h33.html.

2. Frederick M. Hess, "Introduction," in *With the Best of Intentions: How Philanthropy Is Reshaping K–12 Education,* ed. Frederick M. Hess (Cambridge, MA: Harvard Education Press, 2005).

3. Frederick M. Hess, "Re-tooling K–12 Giving," *Philanthropy Magazine,* September–October 2004, http://www.philanthropyroundtable.org/topic/excellence_in_philanthropy/re-tooling_k-12_giving.

4. Jay P. Greene, "Buckets into the Sea: Why Philanthropy Isn't Changing Schools, and How It Could," in *With the Best of Intentions: How Philanthropy Is Reshaping K–12 Education*, ed. Frederick M. Hess (Cambridge, MA: Harvard Education Press, 2005), 77.

5. Frederick M. Hess, *Revolution at the Margins: The Impact of Competition on Urban School Systems* (Washington, DC: Brookings Institution Press, 2002).

Chapter 16

1. TakePart, "About the Film," *Waiting for Superman,* http://www.takepart.com/waiting-for-superman.

2. Frederick M. Hess, "Waiting for Superman: My Conversion Experience," *Education Week,* September 22, 2010, http://blogs.edweek.org/edweek/rick_hess_straight_up/2010/09/waiting_for_superman_my_conversion_experience.html.

3. Jason Felch, Jason Song, and Doug Smith, "Who's Teaching L.A.'s Kids?" *Los Angeles Times,* August 14, 2010, http://articles.latimes.com/2010/aug/14/local/la-me-teachers-value-20100815.

4. Frederick M. Hess, "*LAT* on Teacher Value-Added: A Disheartening Replay," *Education Week*, August 17, 2010, http://blogs.edweek.org/edweek/rick_hess_straight_up/2010/08/lat_on _teacher_value-added_a_disheartening_replay.html.

Chapter 17

1. Pew Research Center, "Political Polarization in the American Public: How Increasing Ideological Uniformity and Partisan Antipathy Affect Politics, Compromise and Everyday Life," June 12, 2014, http://www.people-press.org/2014/06/12/political-polarization-in-the-american-public/.
2. Jesse Graham, Brian A. Nosek, and Jonathan Haidt, *The Moral Stereotypes of Liberals and Conservatives: Exaggeration of Differences across the Political Divide*, April 5, 2012, http://faculty .virginia.edu/haidtlab/articles/manuscripts/graham.nosek.submitted.moral-stereotypes-of -libs-and-cons.pub601.pdf.

Chapter 18

1. Government Printing Office, *Congressional Record* 147, Pt. 6 (May 14, 2001), 7949.
2. Jonah Edelman, "This Issue Is Bigger Than Just Testing," *Education Next* 16, no. 4 (2016), http://educationnext.org/this-issue-is-bigger-than-just-testing-forum-edelman/.
3. Kelly Wallace, "Parents All Over U.S. 'Opting Out' of Standardized Student Testing," *CNN, April 24, 2015,* http://www.cnn.com/2015/04/17/living/parents-movement-opt-out-of-testing-feat /index.html.

Chapter 19

1. Frederick M. Hess, *The Same Thing Over and Over* (Cambridge, MA: Harvard University Press, 2010).
2. Frederick M. Hess, "Tear Down This Wall: The Case for a Radical Overhaul of Teacher Certification," *Educational Horizons* 80, no. 4 (2002), https://www.jstor.org/stable/42927125?seq =1#page_scan_tab_contents.
3. Commission on the Reorganization of Secondary Education, "The Cardinal Principles of Secondary Education," ed. Melissa Scherer, https://www3.nd.edu/~rbarger/www7/cardprin .html.
4. "Duncan Pushes Back on Attacks on Common Core Standards," US Department of Education, June 25, 2013, http://www.ed.gov/news/speeches/duncan-pushes-back-attacks -common-core-standards/.
5. Plato, *The Republic*, trans. Allan Bloom (New York: Basic Books, 1986), 54–55.
6. "Historians Politely Remind Nation to Check What's Happened in Past Before Making Any Big Decisions," *The Onion*, September 28, 2011, http://www.theonion.com/article/historians -politely-remind-nation-to-check-whats-h-26183.

Chapter 20

1. Tom Wolfe, *The Bonfire of the Vanities* (New York: Picador, 2008), 398.

Chapter 21

1. David French, "How to Live a Life of Privilege," *National Review*, May 17, 2014, http://www .nationalreview.com/article/378157/how-live-life-privilege-david-french.
2. Dick Friedman, "Murphy Time," *Harvard Magazine*, November/December 2015, http:// harvardmagazine.com/2015/11/murphy-time.

3. Pew Research Center, "Political Polarization in the American Public: How Increasing Ideological Uniformity and Partisan Antipathy Affect Politics, Compromise and Everyday Life," June 12, 2014, http://www.people-press.org/2014/06/12/political-polarization-in-the-american -public/.

4. Ryan Holiday, "Passion Is the Problem, Not the Solution," Thought Catalog, October 26, 2014, http://thoughtcatalog.com/ryan-holiday/2014/10/passion-is-the-problem-not-the -solution/.

Acknowledgments

I'm indebted to the many people who helped make this book possible. First and foremost, I'd like to offer my heartfelt thanks to the talented Jenn Hatfield for her indispensable role. Jenn was more than a research assistant; her suggestions, management skills, and editorial feedback made her an invaluable partner. I owe an additional vote of thanks to her colleagues Grant Addison, Sarah DuPre, Elizabeth English, Kelsey Hamilton, and Paige Willey, as well as to all-star interns Annie Burch and Matthew Reade.

I also benefited from the suggestions and insights of countless friends and associates. All the students I've taught, staff I've mentored, colleagues with whom I've worked, and opponents I've debated can probably lay claim to anything here that's useful. I especially want to acknowledge a handful of friends who were kind enough to offer comments on early drafts of the manuscript. So my heartfelt thanks to Max Eden, Ashley Jochim, Mike McShane, Jacob Pactor, Julia Rafal-Baer, Carolyn Sattin-Bajaj, Juliet Squire, and Tracey Weinstein.

I owe a special debt to Jal Mehta, Harvard professor, smart guy, and all-around pal. In addition to providing terrific feedback on the manuscript, Jal was the guy who gave me the idea for this book in the first place. It was January 2015. We were having lunch at Legal Seafood in Harvard Square. I told him that I wanted to share what I'd learned from a quarter-century in and around school reform; I thought it was a timely topic but had no clue how to tackle it in an engaging or readable way. Jal thought for a moment, then, in his unhurried manner, he casually suggested, "How about writing letters to a young education reformer?" And here we are. I hope I've done justice to his suggestion. (If not, I trust we can all agree to blame Jal.)

As ever, I owe the deepest appreciation to the American Enterprise Institute and its president, Arthur Brooks, for the support that allows me to call things as I see them, without fear or favor. I know of few places where I'd enjoy the autonomy, intellectual freedom, and remarkable colleagues that AEI has provided me for the past fifteen years. I'm privileged to call it home.

I also want to thank the terrific team at Harvard Education Press. I've had the honor of publishing with HEP for well over a decade, and the relationship is one I cherish. I want to offer particular thanks to HEP editor-in-chief Caroline Chauncey for her faith in this project and fantastic editorial suggestions, and to both Caroline and publisher Doug Clayton for their unwavering friendship and support.

I'm once again indebted to my wife, Joleen, for her love, understanding, and droll editorial advice. These have buoyed me on this project, as on so many others. I'm grateful to my boys for all the laughs, annoyances, and distractions that keep things in perspective. And I'm grateful to my parents for more than I can say (including to my dad for his stalwart copyediting).

Finally, it should go without saying that all the mistakes, flaws, and inanities in these pages are mine and mine alone, while all the good stuff was stolen from a quarter-century's worth of mentors, friends, and colleagues. But as Kurt Vonnegut Jr. would have explained, "So it goes."

About the Author

An educator, political scientist, and author, **Frederick M. Hess** studies K–12 and higher education issues as director of education policy studies at the American Enterprise Institute. His books include *The Cage Busting Teacher, Cage-Busting Leadership, Education Unbound, The Same Thing Over and Over, Common Sense School Reform, Revolution at the Margins*, and *Spinning Wheels*. He authors the popular *Education Week* blog *Rick Hess Straight Up* and is a regular contributor to *The Hill*. His work has appeared in scholarly and popular outlets such as *Teachers College Record, Harvard Education Review, Social Science Quarterly, Urban Affairs Review, American Politics Quarterly, Chronicle of Higher Education, Phi Delta Kappan, Educational Leadership, U.S. News & World Report, The Atlantic, National Affairs, National Review, USA Today, Washington Post, New York Times*, and *Wall Street Journal*. He has edited influential volumes on topics including the Common Core, education philanthropy, the impact of education research, school spending, and No Child Left Behind.

He serves as executive editor of *Education Next*, as senior fellow for the Leadership Institute of Nevada, and on the review board for the Broad Prize for Public Charter Schools. He also serves on the boards of directors of the National Association of Charter School Authorizers and 4.0 SCHOOLS. A former high school social studies teacher, he teaches or has taught at the University of Virginia, the University of Pennsylvania,

Georgetown University, Rice University and Harvard University. He holds an MA and PhD in government, as well as an MEd in teaching and curriculum, from Harvard University.

He lives in Arlington, Virginia, with his wife, Joleen, and their two sons.

Index

Mann, Horace, 129
marriage equality, 81, 82
math instruction, 73
math scores, 51, 53–54
McAdams, Don, 145
meaningless words, 41
media, 107–113
medical research, 64
merit pay, 67–68
messaging, 109
metrics, 49–55
Microsoft, 95
Milwaukee, 89–90
moneyball, 53–54
"My Brother's Keeper" initiative, 46

negative evaluations, 26
Newark, New Jersey, 99–100
New Orleans, 90
new schools, 89
New Schools for New Orleans, 90
New Teacher Project, 25, 110
9/11, 6
90-10 rule, 138
No Child Left Behind (NCLB), 7–8, 51, 59, 71, 73
"No Excuses" charter schools, 39

Obama, Barack, 46, 71, 72–73, 115
Obama administration, 57
Ogston, Rick, 87–88
One Size Does Not Fit All: A Student's Assessment of School (Goya), 3
online materials, 97
"opt-out" movement, 124–125
outcome measures, 51–55
oversight, of charter schools, 90–91

Page, Scott, 21–22
parents, 43–48, 91, 121–126, 151–152
passion, 141–147
people
    judging for yourself, 39–40
    presuming good intentions of, 139
    talking to vs. at, 151
performance metrics, 3, 51–55

persistence, 51
perspective, 39
philanthropy, 99–106
pilot programs, 145–146
Plato, 47, 131–132
Plessy v. Ferguson, 83
policy. *See* education policy
policy debates, 40
politics, 84, 115–119
power, 59–60, 61
predictions, 34–35
pre-K education, 67
printing press, 95
professionalism, 151
progressives, 115–119
push-polls, 76

race-conscious policies, 117
Race to the Top, 30, 57, 58, 73, 74, 105
racial diversity, 22
radio, 94
randomized control trials (RCTs), 65
Ravitch, Diane, 8
reading scores, 51, 53–54
reform
    big-R vs. little-r, 10–11
    challenges of, 4
    changes in, 7
    court-driven, 79–84
    educators and, 13–17
    effectiveness of, 9
    evolution of, 1–11
    history of, 127–133
    launching of new, 60–61
    meaning of, 1, 9
    parenthood and, 121–126
    politics of, 115–119
    proponents of, 76
    pushback to, 74–75
    successes of, 150
reformers
    career advice for, 135–140
    passion and, 141–147
    teachers and, 13–17
research, 63–69, 149–150
Rhee, Michelle, 110–111